DARE
to be
DELIBERATE

DARE
to be
DELIBERATE

LEVEL UP YOUR
COMMUNICATIONS CAREER

ANGEE LINSEY

AVIVA
PUBLISHING
New York

Published by Aviva Publishing

Lake Placid, NY
518-523-1320
www.avivapubs.com

ISBN 978-1-947937-77-2

Cover design by: Carrie Byrne
Book pagination by: Meredith Lindsay/mediamercantile.com
Editor: Joanna Bender

A MESSAGE TO READERS

To communications leaders and those who aspire to be, join the conversation at
#D2bD

ACKNOWLEDGEMENTS

First, I must thank the communications executives who took time to speak with me to share their stories, their wisdom and their sage advice. Their wise words fill these pages and I am honored they felt this project was worthy of their time.

The leaders who landed on these pages are only a drop in the bucket when it comes to where all of the insights shared have originated. To the dozens and dozens of marketing and communications executives I talk to every day about hiring and being hired, thank you for engaging beyond a typical recruiting call.

Thank you to my editor, now friend, Joanna Bender, who was able to take my original manuscript and shape it into a book worth reading. Since journalism school I always believed that you are only as good as your editor, and Joanna made me look good!

An important outcome of writing this book was the Dare to be Deliberate workshop, website and promotional assets. Taking this program and polishing the look and feel is owed to marketer extraordinaire, Carrie Byrne. Her work is beautiful and I recommend her highly.

And thank you to my sister, Lori Hahn and my friend, Kelley Haggert. The two of you have always been there to "take a quick look," give feedback, make suggestions, provide a reality check and generally make this and everything I write or present better for public consumption. I can't tell you how much I appreciate that ongoing support.

And speaking of family, thank you to my parents who have encouraged me from the sidelines and promised to be the first to purchase my book, even though we all know they get free copies.

Finally, for those who inspired and supported me along the way – Kris Plachy and her "She is Relentless" tribe. While at her women's retreat in Hawaii, the D2bD concept was born; Stacey Jaudon, for being one of my dearest friends for decades and introducing me to Joanna; Teri Citterman for encouraging me to take this author journey; Tracy Imm for reminding me that I needed to just get it done; Heidi Trotta and Vic Beck for their wisdom as executives in this field; Kristin Six for adding her wisdom to my workshops; Kelli Nicholas for being my right hand recruiting partner and Christine Pierson for being on my team for so many years (and remaining a key supporter while building her own business); and the Ballard Book Club Babes (past and present), all of whom are dear to me.

I'm sure there are more and once printed, I'll wish I included others. My community is amazing and I know that my life is rich because of the people in it. Thanks to you all!

WHAT PEOPLE ARE SAYING

"This book is incredibly valuable for those who are at the upper-middle management level and considering a move—either because they see others making the leap to VP or CCO and feel left behind or they feel stuck and don't know why they can't make the leap or what it will take to do it successfully.

Anyone at the senior leader level can also leverage this book as a tool in mentoring relationships, and, quite frankly, they may benefit from a little reflection and consideration of their own path to date and what (if anything different) they should do now.

Angee provides candid, insightful anecdotes and advice from a diverse set of senior communicators, as well as from her deep experience as a career coach and executive recruiter. This book is a wonderful extension of her passionate commitment to helping others realize their success."

– Kelley Haggert, VP Communications

"*This book is simply outstanding! What strikes me the most about the book is that Angee covers so many facets of how best to navigate a successful comms career. It's the first time I've looked at strategies and tactics in a completely different way. She lays out the 'why' when it comes implementing a meaningful job path. More importantly, I love how she shows the value of having mentors and champions along the way. Even a seasoned PR pro like myself benefits from the broad overview this book offers those who are about advancing their careers. I can't image going after any position in the future without some type of consultation from Angee.*"

– Ed Stewart, Communications Executive

"*Angee speaks the language of communications. She understands what it takes to be successful in this field and shares these tips in Dare to be Deliberate. As a recruiter she has found incredible talent for me at the mid and senior leader level in two different organizations. Not only does she know how to find who I need, she understands what motivates candidates to make a good career move.*"

– Caroline Shaw, Executive Vice President, Jackson Family Wines

"*Reading this book was like having dinner with a collection of amazing friends. Angee embodies the art of building a powerful network and she sets the bar for how our professional community can support, develop, and empower one another. Whether as a recruiter, coach, connector, or friend, Angee is a champion in the highest degree.*"

– Kristin Graham, Head of Global Employee Communications, Amazon Web Services

"Communications professionals looking for real-world, authentic career advice now have a 'must read' in Angee Linsey's Dare to be Deliberate. You'd be hard pressed to find another single resource with straight talk from communications leaders at the top of their fields — especially in such a concise and well organized format. This book is something I wished I'd had years ago as I entered mid- and senior-level communications roles. Sage counsel from Angee and her contributors abounds, for those who Dare to be Deliberate."

– Mark Dollins, President, Northstar Communications Consulting

"Angee did a masterful job capsulizing all the great advice I've ever received (including from her!) about building a meaningful PR career. Her insights, coupled with real world anecdotes from some of the Communications practice luminaries, make this guide a must-read for mid-level PR professionals interested in advancing their careers."

– Noreen Pratscher, Chief Communications Officer
  and Vice President, Corporate Communications,
  Serta Simmons Bedding, LLC

"Having attended Angee's workshops and talks a number of times, as well as getting her timely coaching, I believe this book offers a treasure trove of great personal perspectives, quotables from trusted communication leaders, and bite-sized digestible morsels of advice that a communicator can use to be deliberate in their career.

This book can and should be required reading for:
- *Young communicators look for inspiration and a roadmap to their strategic success*

- *Seasoned communicators who find themselves in rut and need some "words of wisdom"*
- *Mentors and coaches who are in need a structured framework to have guided supportive conversation with mentees."*

– Derrick Larane, Managing Partner,
  Local Wisdom and Resource Hero

"This is a critical guide for any communications professional who wants a "seat at the table." Use it to break out of the middle of the pack and secure your executive role as a strategically-minded leader. Angee Linsey has provided a lot of actionable wisdom with "Dare To Be Deliberate."

– Hanson Hosein, Director, University of Washington
  Communication Leadership master's program

A quick but powerful read. Universities do a good job preparing graduates for the workforce, but professionals are left to learn "on the job" how to navigate their own careers. Thank you Angee Linsey for shining a bright spotlight on this critically important discipline and providing professionals with a 'user's manual' to nurture and advance their careers.

– Steven Smith, Strategic Global External
  Communications Leader

CONTENTS

INTRODUCTION

Careers are often winding roads that twist and turn. Sometimes you have a map and know exactly where you are going, and other times you have cruise control on, mindlessly traveling down the highway.

And sometimes you just get stuck. Stuck because the forces around you are blocking the way or stuck in your head, unable to see the way forward.

I've worked in communications for three decades, doing everything from journalism to corporate communications and public affairs. About 10 years ago, I founded Linsey Careers, a boutique executive search firm that specializes in marketing and communications recruitment. I have had the pleasure of working with some exceptional professionals at the mid-to-senior and executive levels within this field, hearing their stories, successes and struggles.

In those stories, there are patterns of behavior that make some people's career journey to the top levels of communications leadership seem effortless. And I see patterns where many excellent communications professionals just can't seem to break past a certain point.

That's where the idea for this book came to me.

There seems to be a ton of advice out there for new college graduates. Everyone wants to help junior team members set off on the right foot in their career. What you don't see as often is guidance for those who have established a good beginning—and even middle of their career—but are finding that the view to the top isn't quite as clear as they hoped it would be as they gained great experience as communications practitioners.

It's at that 10-15+ years, post-college stage where so many communicators I interview are seeking ways to move up, gain leadership experience and earn their seat at the table. The road from solid tactician to strategic leader is not always clearly marked.

You feel like you are doing all the right things from a learning and development standpoint—you attend annual conferences and continue to build your technical skills—your head is down and you're working hard. But you admit you haven't really made time to nurture your network.

Maybe there were times you didn't step up for that stretch assignment out of fear or uncertainty that you could handle the job. Or maybe you simply weren't paying close enough attention to your own career development until it was nearly too late.

If you find yourself hovering in the middle with a desire to be more intentional about your career as a communications leader, this book is for you.

There are four key themes that weave throughout this book.

1. **How to keep developing as a practitioner and leader** –This includes internal and external resources, as well as selecting the right opportunities and the right leaders to help you.

2. **How to build trust** – This is particularly important at the executive level, so that you are seen and operating as someone who deserves a seat at the table.

3. **How to effectively move from tactical expert to strategic partner** – This matters for all things communications and growth.

4. **How to transition successfully every step of your career** – This is about always being ready for bigger and better challenges and being the type of leader who is a champion for the top performers on your team.

I will give you some of my own perspectives as an executive recruiter and career coach, as well as share a bit from several well-respected communications executives *through their own voices.*

You will be able to take the stories and lessons and apply them directly to the deliberate evolution of your own career.

It was a tough decision as to which executives I should interview for this book. My criterion was diversity—in gender, race, industry, location, and types of organizations. Each person needed to be a great communications practitioner at the executive level and a great people leader.

I was greeted with tremendous enthusiasm and support for this book—the people I interviewed are passionate about helping the professionals coming up behind them be successful because that is, after all, one of the marks of being a great leader. It is my sincere hope that you will find this book inspiring and helpful as you move forward in your career.

If you are a mid- to senior-level communications professional ready to be more intentional about managing your career or would like to be on my radar screen for potential career opportunities, email me at info@linseycareers.com to schedule your Complimentary 2nd Opinion Career Strategy Session today.

Here's to your success!

Angee Linsey
The Candid Yet Compassionate Career Coach

CHAPTER 1
Shift From Tactical To Strategic

Most communications professionals spend the first few years of their career honing their tactical skills—writing, pitching, creating digital content, implementing internal and external communications initiatives, doing social media campaigns, etc. All these tactical skills are essential to have in your toolbox.

When I speak with candidates, I can tell you with certainty that everyone *thinks* they are strategic. They could be one year out of college and still talk about their strategic leadership.

I'm not saying it isn't possible, but I am saying that most people are building their tactical muscles during the first several years into their career. Sure, they may be contributing to the strategic plans, but far fewer are leading strategy.

Those who truly make this shift from tactical to strategic are the ones who move into the top jobs within communications. Most who make that shift have had exceptional leadership, guidance and great examples of what it could and should look like to be a strategic communications leader.

REAL WORLD LESSONS: BIG-PICTURE THINKING

My journey from tactical to strategic began at Aetna. The company was going through a turnaround, and I was given a new assignment to lead internal communications.

Up until this point, my communications experience had been singularly focused on external communications—focused on reactive media response and promotion of new products and services.

Making the transition and working directly with the President and other members of the C-suite, there was an expectation that the communications would be aligned with the company's strategic priorities, operations and financial performance. I was sitting in meetings where business leaders were visualizing the future direction of the business.

I learned by observing. They weren't talking about the day-to-day tasks that needed to be done—they were seeing end results of planned projects and their potential impact to the company's turnaround. I learned how to adjust my thinking and develop communication programs that integrated with the business priorities.

In essence, I learned how to report on and message internally about our business in a way that elevated actions, programs and successes to align with the C-suite's vision.

I help others make the transition by providing them with context. I think it's important to start any project or assignment with the right context—what are we trying to achieve, what's the goal, what do we want the coverage to say, what's the headline.

This exercise helps my team members think big-picture as opposed to the tasks required to achieve the result. I also think it's important to break strategy into phases by

setting milestones. It helps team members progress and stay motivated.

– Ann Marie Gothard

The Arthur W. Page Society Model

The Arthur W. Page Society is widely recognized as the world's leading professional association for senior public relations and corporate communications executives and educators. The membership criteria are strict, such as corporate members holding the top comms position for companies generating at least $2 billion in annual revenue. Requirements like these ensure the group reflects the "best and brightest" of the profession.

Since several of the executives I interviewed for this book are members of this organization, it seemed a good place to find a working model of how to go about being more strategic.

If you search the internet for a definition of strategic communications, there are literally hundreds, if not thousands, of articles and postings. Here's a well-known and much-debated one from Kirk Hallahan, et al, that was developed from a panel discussion at the International Communications Association:

"The purposeful use of communication by an organization to fulfill its mission." [1]

This is a pretty simplistic explanation, for sure. I'm not going to get into whether I agree or disagree with the authors' definition or their accompanying descriptions of the disciplines involved in assessing an organization's communications. What I do want to draw attention to here is the use of the word "purposeful" because that is a quality that separates strategy from tactics.

Nowhere is "purposeful use" displayed better than the comprehensive model around corporate character that The Arthur W. Page Society presents for effective strategic communications.

Figure 1: The Page Model
– Activating Corporate Character and Authentic Advocacy

"The Page Model begins with the concept of 'Corporate Character,' the definition and alignment of mission, purpose, values, culture, business model, strategy, operations and brand to create the unique, differentiating identity of the enterprise. The organization must authentically embody that character in every interaction to be deserving of trust.

Then, to earn trust with stakeholders, the CCO, using insights derived from behavioral and cognitive science, follows the Authentic Advocacy portion of the model. This starts with building Shared Belief, which then leads decision-makers to take Action on the basis of those beliefs (e.g., to make a purchase, invest their money, accept a job offer, support policy objectives, etc.). Consequently, confidence is built as their actions lead to positive outcomes.

Advocacy at Scale is achieved by empowering individuals to share their experiences with others. Through consistent, authentic engagement, individuals become advocates, which begins the cycle again as shared belief is built with new stakeholders, leading to more actions." [2]

So, how does the work you do measure up to this model?

Obviously, the level where you are right now will impact just how strategic you are able to be in your position. But I would argue that if the entire communications team had a strategic perspective like the one outlined in this model, all the communications activities would point back to that ever-important concept of being aligned with the business goals.

"One time I invited a CEO of a major Bay Area company to a dinner party with some of the best Chief Communications Officers in the area. This CEO had only witnessed tactical level communications support.

I guided the conversation so that the communications executives could paint a picture of what was possible and discuss how other CEOs had missed a story or missed a chance to speak up. The result was that the CEO hired one of the people at that table. Within a short period of time, that new CCO was credited with helping secure a $1 billion win for the company.

Any CEO who doesn't understand the value that comms can bring should sit down with their peers who have experienced first-hand the difference in business results when you have a strong communications leader on the team."

– John Onoda

Demonstrate the Value

Sometimes shifting to a strategic level can be influenced by how an organization views communications as a function. A shocking number of people I speak with say their company does not value the function in a way that gives them the opportunity to be part of the business leadership team.

Edward R. Murrow, the first director of the U.S. Information Agency, famously said after being called in to help with damage control of the 1961 invasion at the Bay of Pigs, "If they want me to be in on the crash landings, I better damn well be involved in the take offs."

It's during a crisis that communications can earn the trust and respect of an executive team quickly. But what about the daily decisions that affect customers, employees, shareholders, and the community where your business is located?

The short answer is, you must demonstrate strategic value in the daily "take offs" to be considered for a seat at the executive table. It's through proving value that you create a context for communications and earn trust from the organization's leadership.

It's been my experience as a coach and a recruiter that communications professionals often wrestle with *how* to remind their organizations of their value. You also have to remind people *consistently*, as in every day, of the value you bring.

"To be seen as strategic and essential, we have to get away from thinking no one can do without us. We have to redefine our value to the organization. We're not just collaborating with the CEO and C-suite, but we are looking at how teams operate across business functions.

I don't define communications by talking about media relations, internal communications, social media—that's a tactical conversation. Instead, I focus more on reputation and risk management.

I talk about how strategic communications is really an enabler for reaching the appropriate stakeholders. We are engaging the right people to move the organization forward. I focus on what the function can do vs. what are the tools in the toolbox.

I am more adept now at looking at the work I do in communications with a business lens. I have become a better business leader because of my role working with the chair and CEO of a $65 billion organization and watching how he thinks, acts and does."

– Donna Uchida

Recently, I was speaking with a mid-level communications professional who we will call "Emily." She was looking to move from her current title of senior manager to director.

My first question was, "What are you doing differently that makes your role worthy of the title increase in the minds of the leadership team?"

Emily began to answer with a series of tactical initiatives that she has accomplished in recent months. As I probed on how those initiatives aligned with the organization's business goals, she couldn't really answer the question. I asked if she knew what the organization's goals were. Again, no answer.

We then talked about what were her boss's priorities. She had never had that conversation with her boss.

It turned out that Emily was seen in her company as a tactical. Maybe even simply an order taker. She wasn't asked to sit in on the meetings to create solutions because she was seen as the person to communicate whatever was already decided.

For Emily, I encouraged her to have a career conversation with her boss to quickly identify what mattered most to her and to those with whom she reports. What were her priorities? What were the priorities of the executive leadership team?

By simply asking those questions, Emily will be seen positively by any good leader.

From there, she could start reporting back on the work that she is doing from the lens of the business priorities.

It's one thing to say your PR efforts landed you a positive story in the *Wall Street Journal*. It's another to say how that story was a targeted effort aligned to specific objectives the company was seeking to achieve.

If you aren't already doing it, the first step in being strategic is to speak the language of the business. Consistently align the work you are doing with the business goals. Tell the story of what you and your team are doing — not just with tactics, but with measurable results.

How you tell the story—which should be early and often—will be the key to showing your leadership team that communications, and you, are part of the strategic solution to business success.

"If all you do is take orders and not seek to truly understand what business leaders are trying to accomplish, you will be viewed as the poster maker or press release writer.

You must be fearless. You have to be comfortable driving to do what's right for the business, and you need to understand the business to be effective in doing that.

Sometimes the boss will want you to do something a certain way and sometimes you have to do it that way, but you still have to push back when you know what's right."

– Michelle Jones

Letting Go Of What You Know

When you're moving from tactical to strategic, you have to let go of things you know how to do. You can't do everything.

To be a truly strategic leader, you have to ask yourself constantly, "What value am I adding?" and keep your focus on things that matter.

I knew a woman who, when she became a VP, also became a magnet for everyone's problems. She tried to fix all of them, and it was a recipe for disaster!

She had to keep reminding herself that she was turning into something other than the version of herself that the president hired. She was put in the role to create and lead the organization, and the only way that was going to happen would be if she cut some old umbilical cords—then she could become successful and move the company forward.

It's really hard to let go of what you know, and it's even harder to let go knowing that there's a good chance you're training someone to eventually take over your position. But it's an important part of the journey toward becoming more strategic.

"It was amazing when I realized I didn't need to know everything. I had to keep focused on setting direction, doing individual work and intervening to support the team.

There was a time when I could scale and know every feed-speed of a product, or every detail on a refreshed algorithm, or the setup for social media listening and sentiment monitors. Today, I can't scale that deep, but I can hire the best people who can do those things and lead in areas I do not have enough time to spend in."

–Krista Todd

◀ Remember This!

Have you made the shift from tactical to strategic? There is always room for growth, regardless of where you are in your career, so why not have a career conversation with your boss and mentors to identify your gaps and start working toward filling them?

You can begin preparing for those conversations with a bit of self-reflection:

- How much of your week is currently focused on tactical execution of communications plans and activities?

- Are you an order taker or do you take a consultative approach with the leadership team regarding how they can best achieve their goals through solid communications strategies?

- How often are you leading the conversation around how communications can help the organization achieve a specific goal or the broader business objectives?

- When you are at the table during any business conversation, what do you contribute to the conversation? How are your ideas received? How do you follow up with specific actions?

- When speaking with your boss or mentors, discuss your observations of where you are currently and check in with them to see if your perception matches theirs.

- Where there are gaps, ask for support to gain opportunity to stretch your strategic muscles. If your gaps require training or more specific guidance, create an action plan to help get you to the next level within a designated time period.

CHAPTER 2
Develop Your Business Skills

Virtually every interview I conducted for this book included the value of broader experience beyond straight marketing and communications if you want to secure the top job and a seat at the executive table. Some of the most often mentioned were:

- Speak the language of the business
- Sit in on those earning calls
- Stay current on industry news and general current events that could affect your industry
- Seek ways to measure your communications programs against the outcomes the business is trying to achieve
- Ask to sit at the executive table if you have not been invited, and, once there, deliver
- Invite feedback consistently and pay attention to it

Chances are, if you are at the mid-to-senior level of your career, you have had a chance to develop your overall business skills to some degree. But it's a never-ending process.

Speak the Language of the Business

Communications professionals are specialists, and there's no doubt that they see the world through a unique lens.

Knowing who the audiences are, knowing what messages to craft for them, and knowing when the right moment is to share the news are all important skills that the best practitioners have.

However, to help secure your seat at the top, it's wise to learn the "language of the business." This means widening and deepening your knowledge base so that you have a good understanding of what impacts the business.

This would include items such as:

- Profit and loss statements
- Sales KPIs
- Competitor strengths/challenges
- Risk management

In short, you want to do your communications job through the framework of business. You want to look at your job and the value you bring through the eyes of your CEO and executive leadership team. What do they see and what are the items that capture their attention?

"We are specialists as communicators, and we see things differently. But to earn a seat at the table, the first thing we need is to speak the language of the business. Know the numbers. Be clear who your audiences are. Know what your boss cares about so you are up-to-speed on those issues. I regularly check in with my boss and ask him or her one question, "What keeps you up at night?"

You can talk all day long about great story telling and

results of a campaign, but I've never found a better way to get to the heart of what matters to the boss. It gives you the insight as a communicator how what you do can, and should have, a role in helping solve those issues."

–Jason Hunke

Sit In on Earning Calls

Understanding how your company makes and spends money doesn't require you to be a financial expert. But to speak the language of the business, you need a general understanding of these things.

If you work for a public company, sitting in on earnings calls will definitely make you smarter about the business. Here are a few tips to make the call more meaningful:

- Prep before the call – Go back and listen to the previous call or read the transcript. Do some homework on what analysts were saying and look at the stock prices and company performance over that quarter. Take note of the benchmarks and metrics used by Wall Street, the industry and your company.

- Read the earnings release – These releases typically are issued about an hour or so prior to the call and can be found on the company website. Review those stated benchmarks and metrics and pay attention to announcements for the future. When looking at the balance sheet, focus on changes in financial position.

- Listen to the call – These calls are open to the entire public—it's the law. There's a common format to the call including a Q&A at the end.

- Analyze the earnings call – I encourage you to sit down with your boss to discuss what you learned on the call and the market's reaction after the call. Ask questions about the areas you may not have fully understood. Find out how to participate in the communications efforts for the next earnings call.

If you work for a privately held company or non-profit organization, there is still an opportunity to get knowledgeable about the financials of the company.

For example, you can ask to join a development committee meeting, where the fundraising team spends time analyzing data about prospective donors. Or sit in for an afternoon with the grant writer, as they're collecting and presenting information for the next grant proposal.

This goes back to being part of the business and paying attention to where and how money is being earned and spent. When you know the company's financial priorities, you have a better business perspective.

"A good way to gain credibility is to get a broader exposure within the function and the organization. Do a stint in financial communications or work on the analyst reports. You can't be CCO of a public company if you aren't familiar with SEC or NYSE rules.

Another way to have a broader business mindset is by getting an MBA instead of a master's in communications. Or serve time in a line of business and own a P&L. Nothing gets you more credibility than having a P&L."

– John Onoda

Stay Current on Industry News and General Current Events

Communications professionals with a broader exposure to information are consistently identified by the people I interviewed for this book as successors for the top jobs.

That means you need to be a reader of trade news, world news, financial news, etc.—not just news that is directly related to communications, or even just your industry.

One way to build on your business knowledge is to pick up the *Wall Street Journal* and read all the sections—all the columns, all the industry and financial news, everything.

When you do that, you get a good glimpse inside the head of a CEO, since chances are they have read the Wall Street Journal every day for the last 20 years. There's a whole vocabulary and mindset that has been cultivated by that practice.

Most CEOs can tell in about 30 seconds who thinks like an executive—it's the person who can step out of his/her own shoes and look at a problem strategically.

Just don't wait until you're at the director level to start the habit because, by then, it's too late!

Measurement Matters

We all know that measuring communications efforts is important. I remember the days when we would talk about PR success by equating column inches of press to advertising dollars for similar space. I'm so glad we've improved our metrics since then.

With so much of our work being done digitally, there are any number of tools to help measure practically everything that you do in communications. What's important is to share that data in a way that helps the organization understand what you're doing and why it matters.

For example, get really good at story telling combined with your metrics for measuring successful communications programs. It doesn't matter if you are sharing this formally during meetings or performance reviews, or more informally during every day conversations.

When you put together a great narrative that allows any listener to see the positive impact communications has on the business, you can develop and sustain the support for the strategic value of communications.

"It's our responsibility to show senior executives how we bring value — that integration, consistency and credibility drive results.

One way to do that is by measuring what you're doing. When communications is a strategic function, it needs to be measured like any other business function. With all the digital tools available today, measurement is easier than ever.

You may be measuring social media engagement, recruiting results based on certain employer brand campaigns, employee pulse surveys. Everything your team is doing needs to show how you are helping the business drive desired results.

Then you can't keep those results a secret! Reporting those results in a way that is understood by the business and the executive leadership team is essential. For example, my teams have sent monthly reports to senior leadership and quarterly to the board that reinforces what we are about, and why we matter to profitable growth."

– Michelle Jones

Ask for Your Seat at the Table

When an organization sees the communications function as a strategic and essential part of the executive team and your participation is valued during the decision-making process, you've got a seat at the table.

But the hard truth is that no one is bestowed that seat—everyone has to earn their own way. And this is not easy, especially given that big communications jobs are high intensity jobs with higher turnover rates—about every 3-4 years.

> "Let's not talk about how we need a seat—take a seat. To do that, if you aren't being invited to key meetings, start asking to sit in. And when invited, speak up. Then most importantly, deliver.
>
> – Krista Todd

If you're not being invited to sit in on strategic meetings, it's time to ask to be included. A "seat at the table" may be different in every organization.

You may be leading communications for a business unit and having a seat at the table with the leadership team of that business unit is where you should be. It doesn't always mean you have to be sitting with the Executive Leadership Team.

That being said, if you have eyes on the top communications job at a company, earning the trust and respect to get to that executive table is essential.

Once you get that seat, be prepared to deliver and contribute *thoughtfully*. Communicators bring a lens that no other functional leader can offer.

You have the view of every stakeholder that will be on the receiving end of every business decision. Those stakeholders may be internal or external—and offering your perspective of how messages will land could have an impact on the decisions themselves.

> "The key to success has nothing to do with your title. It's about influence and making an impact on the business—owning a proverbial seat at the executive table. And it's important to know that when you do get that seat, it might not look like what you'd expected.
>
> Communications leaders should be surfacing threats or problems before they hit the business to help the CEO and executive team make better decisions. That might mean offering perspectives about competitors' movements, or insight into the regulatory or public policy environment, or recommendations about cybersecurity threats.
>
> If I could give advice to CEOs who don't view communications as a C-level function, I would tell them that they should expect more—in fact, they should demand it. If communications isn't a strategic partner to the executive team, they're not getting their money's worth."
>
> – Steve Astle

Invite Feedback Consistently and Pay Attention to It

When you're looking to move up the ranks professionally, a good idea is to talk with people you know who are already there and ask them some questions.

How did they get there? What is it like? What's their advice for you to get there? Having conversations regularly with leaders, mentors and others in your network allows you to be a sponge, ask questions and then put into practice what you learn.

You can also get feedback from the people you work with, either openly or anonymously, through personal leadership surveys and assessments that look at all aspects of you, your strengths and challenges and your overall abilities—the $360°$ view.

It may surprise you what you learn, since we often see ourselves one way and the world sees us another way.

Regardless of how you ask for feedback, the bottom line is that you must have courage to hear it and the commitment to act on it.

"Knowing who you are and where you're going is key to success. You have to build the right relationships from a 360 perspective.

Get candid feedback from peers, people above and below and peripheral to your role in the company. You can even do it anonymously.

When I did this, I didn't know how I was coming across to some people and I took it to heart. I changed my behavior. You must have the courage to correct your wrongs. Be fearless.

You also have to show up every day and be ready to play the game. If you are still taping your ankles when the game starts, you aren't ready to play. As a coach, I'm not putting you in the game.

On the job, if you aren't thinking strategically, I'm going

to relegate you to a certain position. That's unfortunate, and you'll miss out. I'll coach you, but if you don't get the message, eventually you will be gone."

– David Albritton

◀ Remember This!

Developing business skills takes time and effort. You have likely been doing many of these things all along, but sometimes it's a good reminder to never rest on your laurels.

What daily habit can you create to be more broadly aware of how world events may impact your business? Whether it's checking online news sources, listening to local broadcasts or reading trade journals, the ability to "see around corners" is highly valued by the leadership team, and your contribution will help the business from a risk and reputation standpoint.

To be the most effective leader in communications, you must build trust and influence across the organization. This requires getting a seat at the table and, particularly with the leadership team, developing the relationship required to have a meaningful voice when decisions are being made.

CHAPTER 3
Know Yourself

As you make the shift to becoming a strategic leader, it is a critical time to be very thoughtful about your career moves. This can be within your current organization or moving on to another company to get new and more expanded responsibility.

When I have a conversation with a candidate that may result in a career move, I always ask two critical questions:

1. What is (or would need to be) happening in your world to consider a career move?

2. If you could walk into your ideal job right now, what would it look like?

Knowing the answer to both these questions is crucial to being deliberate in your career. The answers are not static year after year. Our lives evolve. Our wants and needs change.

Interestingly, the answers may not always lead you to a new company, but rather to better conversations with your boss.

It Starts with Values

What matters most and least to you in life and work is a great place to start when you are thinking about your career beyond your current job. Otherwise, you may make choices based on criteria that leave you frustrated or just plain miserable.

I hear about people who have taken a role because the money was too good to turn down and the title was what they were looking for, but the company's mission or culture does not align with their values. I've seen people choose the "cachet" of the company or role because it would "look good on a résumé," but the leader was terrible, or the expectations and workload were unreasonable.

Or I've seen others who are with an organization they love, but they have a new boss and they are taking the team in a new direction. Or maybe there is nowhere to go within the company they love. Even worse, there are places to go within the organization, but those opportunities don't seem to be coming their way.

This is when knowing your values makes all the difference.

◀ NOTES FROM ANGEE

I was working with a candidate who I will call "Serena."

Serena had multiple job offers. She was an A-player whose position had been eliminated in a large reorganization—circumstances she had never experienced before.

Naturally, my hope was that she would accept the offer I had presented to her, but I heard loud and clear what she wasn't saying as she evaluated her different opportunities.

Serena had been both a consultant and an in-house communications practitioner with a focus on internal communications. She was well-respected by clients, executives and team members in every role. Having earned a master's degree in organizational leadership and taking roles at prestigious brand name companies, she was very intentional about doing all the "right things" in her career.

But suddenly, she was uncertain. Her priorities had shifted slightly with a young child at home, a husband who was finishing his teaching degree, and a desire to have a life and a job that was fulfilling. She loved the diversity and pace agency life offered yet also enjoyed working within a company to see plans through from beginning to end.

Serena was literally paralyzed with indecision. Each of the choices before her would mean a different path.

My advice to Serena and anyone in this situation? Find a values exercise that really makes you get clear on your what matters most to you. Know your priorities and your fundamental beliefs.

One of my favorites is from Scott Jeffrey. I like this exercise because it doesn't focus on a list of words. Instead, through story telling of your own experiences—both good and bad—you uncover where your values are showing up and where they are woefully absent.[1]

Culture Fit

When recruiting, I work very closely with hiring leaders to ascertain their corporate culture. The easy part of finding candidates is finding the right skills and experience, but the most important part is finding the right cultural fit for the team. Those intangibles are hard to articulate for most leaders—and it's often done with broadly defined words like "creative" or "smart" or "collaborative."

One thing we do to help get clear on those characteristics required to be successful in a specific organization, is to define and describe what those words mean to the leader. We talk about the company's values and how they use those values in everyday business.

Finding an organization that has values that align with yours is the holy grail. That's why starting with *your* values first will make it so much easier to identify companies and teams that are a cultural match for you.

REAL WORLD LESSONS: LOOK FOR THE CULTURE FIT

I've always preached to myself and others, "don't go to a company if you cannot embrace the culture." Some of the moves I've made were like going to different planets.

When I went to GM, I wasn't really a car guy. The corporate culture and Midwestern life was very different than what I and my family had been experiencing in San Francisco roots. My wife and two teenaged children struggled to adjust, and it got to the point where I had to make a choice between my career at GM and the well-being of my family.

It took about ten seconds of deliberation. Within months, we were all back home in California and I was starting a new job at Visa USA.

Sometimes, when you're looking at jobs and talking to a handful of senior executives, you may not be fully attuned to the culture or be able to extrapolate from the interview what the work will be.

Many interviews are bad experiences. The company goes radio silent, or the process is dragged out. Sometimes the person interviewing you is late or maybe doesn't even show up. While we may make excuses for these signs, these are all indicators of the corporate culture.

When I was being considered for an executive role at Levi Strauss, I met with the SVP of Corporate Affairs and we had a three-hour discussion on ethics and values. Not one question about my skills or experience.

The last interview was with the Chairman. When I thanked

him for his time at the end of the interview, he said, "This is the most important thing I'm going to do today."

Those two conversations told me all I needed to know about the company being a culture match.

– John Onoda

"I think when you start answering the mail and not believing in the brand or ethos of the company, you are on a derailment path.

As communicators, we are all about the brand and ethics. How we promote and engage matters. If the company is on a different path than you feel aligned, it's hard to do your job. It's hard to sell what you don't believe.

You may think you are a force to change the entire culture single handedly. When that happens, you know you have to leave, and that's a scary place. But being incongruent and not aligned, that's when things start to derail. You have to make tough choices."

– Michelle Jones

Look at Life a Little Differently

When you're stuck in transition, you look for the job you already have since it's the job you know.

When I was in that bad spot, I would look at jobs and my eyes would glaze over because every job I saw was the same job I was in. I would think, "It's just geography. I'm going to be just as miserable over there as I am here. What am I doing wrong and why is this not working?"

To get out of this tough place, you must have a vision of where you're going. After you establish your values, the next critical step is clarifying your vision.

This isn't easy! I had a lot of ups-and-downs and ins-and-outs getting to where I am professionally. Today, I'm 100% certain I'm in the right spot. You will discover yours, too, and—to prove you're not alone on this journey—I've shared my "vision quest" at the end of this book. (See *About the Author* section.)

One of my favorite activities to do in in my workshops on career change is to ask participants to look around the room and find everything that is the color blue. Look around, lock it in, there will be a quiz. The audience looks earnestly and concentrates on all things blue.

Then I ask them to close their eyes and tell me everything that's yellow!

My point in the workshop is that, when you're looking for a job, "blue" is the job you know, and all the other colors, like yellow or red or green, are the jobs you haven't thought of yet. They may not even appear to your consciousness when scouring job postings or talking about potential career moves.

By writing down what matters to you and not assigning tasks, titles or companies to it, opportunities you hadn't thought of often find their way to you and will make you look at your life differently.

In the back of this book, you'll find a vision exercise that will help you get clear about what matters in your life right now. It will make the "yellow" and other colors start to pop out for you.

You will find out those things that are absolute deal breakers (or deal makers) when it comes to aligning your values with that of the job you hold.

Yes, this exercise is about the power of intention, the law of attraction. What you think about is what comes into view.

◀ **Remember This!**

I'm guessing you have every intention of doing the values and vision exercise… eventually. I want to encourage you to do it today. No really. Today.

I can't tell you how many people told me they started these exercises but didn't make time or space to really think hard about what ideal really looks like.

Sometimes people are *afraid* to consider that they could actually have all of the things they want in life and work. Those people either don't do the exercise at all, or they do it with little thought or ambition.

But I know that's not you. Otherwise, you wouldn't have picked up this book.

So go forth and imagine what would be perfect and write it down as if it's happening. When I did it, I printed the page of sentences and set it aside. Nothing happened—until it did.

Within a year, I was literally doing *every single thing* in my vision. And let me say, I had some pretty bold sentences written down. I've shared this exercise with so many people, and those who did it had similar experiences.

What you think about is what comes into view. And the view from where I sit has gotten really good. Yours can too.

CHAPTER 4
What Qualities Do Leaders Seek?

Quality people are what make a strong communications team. The pain of finding and retaining top talent is felt across every industry and in every region of the country.

As leaders, everyone I spoke with for this book talked about the importance of identifying quality people and ensuring the work was interesting enough to hold on to them.

So, what are executives looking for when identifying high potential members of their team, or when they are hiring at the mid-to-senior levels?

Like everything that involves people, there are no black-and-white answers. But there were several themes that came out when I asked this question.

Actual communications skills rarely came into the discussion, mostly because those are assumed. They are table stakes. But I will say there are strong opinions about the quality of writing (or lack thereof) that is felt throughout the communications community.

To excel in this field, you have to hone your writing skills. You can never stop practicing or be too proud to get help if you need it. It's the cornerstone of this work.

> "I can tell within five minutes of an interview if someone is high potential. They believe in purpose, and they don't stay in one place for a long time. When they aren't adding value, they move on."
>
> –Marta Newhart

Attitude

Attitude and intelligence were touched upon in many conversations, with the best candidates exhibiting both. However, when pressed, most of the leaders I interviewed prefer attitude but acknowledge that "intelligence makes it easier" to succeed.

Having a positive attitude is a given, but the meaning goes beyond being positivity. It's really about being open and willing to take on new challenges. It's about seeking ways to be better and do better. It's eagerness and drive combined with patience and willingness to do the work that will help you grow.

As Zig Ziglar said, "'It is your attitude, more than your aptitude, that will determine your altitude."

Business acumen

As discussed earlier, to truly be a leader, you must know the business and speak the language of the executive team. That includes knowing the numbers.

If you can't articulate how (or why) the business makes money, you've lost the trust at the top.

Business acumen also includes understanding the political

environment of your organization and how to identify what is least and most important to those setting the agenda for the company.

In addition, it is important to be mindful of all the stakeholders. As communicators, every message must be targeted to land with all of the different audiences. Knowing and aligning business goals with how you tell those stories to the various stakeholders is essential.

Courage

Courage comes in many forms. Research professor and author Brené Brown reminds us that "the root of the word *courage* is cor—the Latin word for heart. In its earliest forms, *courage* meant 'to speak one's mind by telling all one's heart.' Today, the word is more synonymous with being heroic."[1]

In the workplace, courage includes having a point of view and being able to articulate it. At every executive meeting where you are presenting a plan or contributing to an important business decision, you have to step up with your unique communicator's point of view.

Another side to courage means not being intimidated when you are presenting those plans to a CEO or other senior executives. That person is not going to mince words—they're usually quite busy and won't have time for a huge explanation—so you must be prepared to answer from an executive perspective.

Of course, there are times that you do have to step away from your position, but for every executive I spoke with, they all reflected on the importance of being willing to stand up for your best ideas, whether they're accepted or not.

"You must have the courage not to be intimidated by high-level people who are asking the right questions based on the decisions they have to make. If you back down, you are dead in the water."

– Donna Uchida

Curiosity

Nearly every hiring leader I have worked with, in addition to the leaders interviewed for this book, has expressed a need for intellectual curiosity as a core competency for success.

That is illustrated through a willingness to explore ideas, cultures and experiences. Reading, keeping up with current events, exploring new ideas—they're ways of being and engaging with the world around you.

Without curiosity, you are limited by the boundaries of your experience when it comes to tackling problems. Many leaders are far less interested in your communications background than in what else you can bring to the table.

"The most successful communications strategy and counsel I've seen come from the minds that are the most curious.

Communications leaders have a responsibility to know the broader world around them and understand deeply the context in which they operate.

Our jobs are then to consistently take that 360-degree world view and boil it down to something relevant and influential."

– Cory Curtis

Emotional Intelligence

Having the ability to recognize our own emotions and those of others is the basis of emotional intelligence. It affects how we manage behavior, navigate social complexities and make personal decisions that achieve positive results.

To rise to the top of any organization, regardless of function, you must have emotional intelligence. It makes you a better leader, allows you to show empathy and is critical for adapting to environments and achieving goals. It helps you handle stressful situations and help others through change.

> "How you can be a buffer says a lot about your leadership abilities, especially in tough environments. Emotional intelligence is at the center of it."
>
> – Jason Hunke

Ethics

As storytellers for the organization, ethical behavior is non-negotiable. Cutting corners and alternative facts have no place for anyone looking for the top communications jobs.

Ethics can also be bundled into the broader conversation around culture fit. Knowing that you are ethically aligned with an organization so that you can sleep well at night and do your best work is not something to take lightly.

Rounding Out The List

Additional characteristics that surfaced during my conversations included executive presence, persuasive, diplomatic, patient, analytical thinker, driven, consistent and listener.

I'm sure there are many more, depending on who you ask.

The goal is to be self-aware. You must know who you are—your values, beliefs, preferences and motivators—and be able to articulate those to your boss or potential new leader.

Ensuring who you are is in alignment with where you are and where you are going is the essence of being deliberate in your career.

◀ Remember This!

Some organizations are very clear about the leadership traits that matter most to them. Amazon goes so far as posting their Leadership Principles in the jobs section of their website.

They advise candidates to learn the principles and come prepared with examples of how they have applied them in their work and life. They interview for those traits, and they measure success on them as well.

What leadership qualities are valued at your organization? In your next career conversation with your boss, talk about the characteristics that matter to him or her. Find out if you are demonstrating those traits at the level needed to continue to move up within your organization. If not, enlist your boss to help you get there. A good leader will welcome the opportunity to help you develop.

CHAPTER 5
Networks, Mentors and Champions

◀

Networking—ugh! I don't know anyone who loves the concept.

The mere mention of the importance of networking conjures up images of rooms full of people passing out business cards and disingenuously promising to stay in touch. That sounds horrible, and, by the way, is usually pretty ineffective.

My approach to networking is really all about having meaningful conversations. For me, this is quality one-on-one time with people you have things in common with, or whom you want to learn something from, or someone you can bring value to because of what you know. It can actually be pretty fun if done right!

Identifying those individuals who you genuinely have a connection with and making it a habit to nurture that relationship over years is a critical part of growing your professional career.

People are so busy managing their jobs and gaining the hard skills that they forget to manage their careers. Suddenly, you're 15 years into it and you need to make a move, but you haven't made time to build relationships with other senior professionals who can help you maneuver through career challenges, guide toward stretch assignments, and land into roles that are a good match.

The time to reach out is not just when you need help. People help you because they know and like you, and that only happens over time.

> "No one tells you during the first half of your career that it is the time you need to be working on the second half of your career.
>
> Sometimes I will meet a senior level communicator at an event and a week later they send me their résumé asking me for help in their job search. I don't have a relationship with that person yet—it's a big ask. I am more likely to help someone I have built a strong foundation over years.
>
> – John Onoda

Know Your Network

A good way to start identifying who is already in your network is to create three lists: acquaintances, allies and champions.

Acquaintances – These are people you have met, and you could call them for information or referrals to resources. Be strategic when identifying who you want to build the relationship in a way with inside this group that moves them into one of the other two categories.

Allies – These are people with whom you have had a good working relationship. You know each other well enough that you could call upon them when you need help with a problem.

Champions – They will recommend you (even without being asked) because they know and respect your work. Champions are sometimes referred to as "advocates."

With social media connecting us to so many people both personally and professionally, it can be confusing what level to assign to people who may only be connected electronically. If you rely on tools like Linked In for your professional network, download a list of your connections and prioritize them.

You will probably find that you have only a handful of champions. Your allies will be a little larger in number, but most people truly fall into the acquaintance category.

And, depending on how you've approached your social network, you may have people "connected" to you that you have never met, so they would not fall into any of these three areas. (Though you could make an effort to move them to the acquaintance file if you reached out.)

Once created, evaluate that chart of your network contacts and create a routine for staying in touch with your allies and champions. How can you be a resource for them? Perhaps create a cadence for just reaching out and saying hello.

Who Are Your Champions?

Champions are people who will advocate for you when you are not in the room. Without you asking, and maybe without you even knowing, they seek ways to open doors for you.

You may have only a few champions in your career. These relationships are special and should never be taken for granted. Think about current or former executives you've worked with, mentors or maybe even a client you've worked with for years. These are likely the people who will be in this category.

When someone considers themselves your champion, they are happy to help you. They want to stay in touch with you to stay current on what you are doing and where you are trying to go in your career.

Never be afraid to reach out to connect on a personal level. You may be a resource for them as well. Don't wait until you need something to reach out. Be willing to stay in touch on a routine basis as well.

> "Champions are people who are willing to put their names and reputations on the line to recommend you for a high-visibility project. Your name may not have even come up in the initial discussion, but they are willing to invest in your success.
>
> Your champions are willing to give you access to doors that don't open without a little help."
>
> – Donna Uchida

Online And Local Connections

Networking is where social media is both a blessing and a curse.

So often we think that "liking" a post is enough to nurture the network. It can help, but why not take a few extra seconds and actually send a private message with a note of congratulations or comment? Maybe share something you have been working on that you know they would find valuable because of their own circumstances.

I'd like to add a side note to the notion of being deliberate in your connections. It absolutely must be authentic. Trust me when I tell you that people can feel it when your outreach has purely selfish motives.

Personal connection is what builds relationships. That, of course, goes beyond social media. So, make time for an occasional coffee or lunch. Connect with acquaintances at conferences and events. Seek out local groups (both formal and informal) that allow you to connect with your peers.

Early in your career, you likely joined organizations like Public Relations Society of America (PRSA) or International Association of Business Communicators (IABC). I'm an active member of both and find them to be rich with content and provide excellent opportunities to mix with other professionals in the field.

Depending on where you live, the local chapters can be tremendous places to strengthen your local network of peers. If you don't have strong local participation, the regional and national conferences may energize you and broaden your network.

If conferences or events are something your company is willing to invest in, other organizations include Ragan Communications, American Marketing Association, Women in Communications, Social Media Association, and many more. Find the ones that bring the most value to you based on what you want to learn and your career goals.

Seeking More Senior Level Peer Groups

But what happens when you move to more senior ranks and you aren't getting the same interaction at the peer level? That is when it's time to up your game when it comes to where you spend your professional development dollars.

Half of the 10 people I interviewed for this book are members of the Arthur W. Page Society. This prestigious organization requires you to be nominated, and you must hold the top Communications job in a $2 billion company or larger. It's exclusive, and their members are among the top communications leaders in the world.

In recent years, they have added Page Up and the Future Leaders programs. These also require sponsorship from members, but, if you are working in an organization that qualifies you to join, it's an amazing opportunity to learn and grow with rich content delivered by exceptional leaders.

"It's not enough to shake hands and get business cards. Networking is an art – find ways to differentiate from other people seeking engagement with that person you want to connect with. If I said something that resonated with you, leverage that and send me a note.

We are all humans and have egos and if you ask me what I do for a living, my ego will ensure I tell you all about myself – and very proudly. Ask for 15 minutes, maybe grab a coffee and genuinely learn who that person is, so you can then share who you are and build a relationship. That's how you begin to build a meaningful network."

– David Albritton

More informal methods of connecting with peer level leaders are through locally grown groups. For example, in Seattle there is the Seattle Internal Communications Leadership Forum (SICLF) that was created by a few Internal Communication leaders who saw the gap and filled it.

A local agency also created a group where CCOs in the area get together for dinner on a regular basis. Its's well-attended because there aren't a lot of opportunities for this executive group to be in one room.

I hear from clients regularly, "Oh yeah.... I really should participate in those things, but I just don't have time."

It must be a priority, or you will find yourself in the middle of your career and simply stuck in the middle.

The World Outside of Communications

Expanding your network outside of the function is also important in any career.

When you have been identified as a high potential employee, you may be put into a leadership program inside your company. This exceptional opportunity to build relationships with other high-potential leaders in multiple disciplines is where you will increase your business acumen and understanding of company goals from new perspectives.

The reality is, your boss may not be focusing on your career development as much as you should be paying attention to it yourself.

Seek out affinity groups and leadership development opportunities both within your organization and outside of it. Get the support of your leaders to demonstrate your interest in being deliberate in your career and your drive to make it happen.

"I've been part of creating a Women's Leadership Network or mentoring circles everywhere I work. Having opportunities to learn and share across functions is a great way to help people grow and it improves retention."

– Ann Marie Gothard

Get Yourself A Mentor

Because leaders build leaders, everyone I interviewed for this book had countless stories about how they value mentoring others, and the lessons they learned from those who mentored them.

Before I share some of those stories, here are a few thoughts on how to find and keep important mentors over your career.

Choose mentors who have leadership characteristics, experience or knowledge you hope to achieve. Many will be within the communications function, but don't limit yourself to only people in your career field. There is much to learn about business from the other disciplines.

- When asking someone to be your mentor, always do it in person. Email may feel easier, but you won't develop the kind of open and honest relationship you want from this approach.

- Pay attention to leaders who are offering their guidance and wisdom. They have chosen you for a reason.

- Know what your expectations are from your mentor and be willing to share those. This will help your mentor feel more comfortable agreeing to help.

- When meeting with your mentor, be prepared with thoughtful questions. Don't go in only as a "taker." Be willing to be a resource to your mentor as well.

- Always express appreciation when your mentor provides time and advice. A quick note of thanks goes a long way.

REAL WORLD LESSONS:
AN INVITATION HE COULDN'T REFUSE

I was working at a major PR firm in San Francisco. One day, an invitation came my way to have lunch with one of the EVPs.

This leader was two levels above me, a very eminent person in our field, and I had no idea why he'd invited me to lunch, but of course I accepted. We had a lovely lunch, talking about everything and nothing—a wide-ranging conversation that, to me, at least, didn't seem to have a clear objective.

At the end of the meal, this executive offered to meet with me more regularly. When I got back to the office, I told a friend about it. I said, 'Can you believe that? Why would he want to have lunch with me?' My friend said, 'You dope! Don't you know what this means? He's offering to mentor you.'

And so it was! That executive was John Onoda, and in the intervening years he's helped me immeasurably by challenging and encouraging me through many tricky situations and by celebrating my successes. He's been enormously generous toward me, and if it weren't for my plain-spoken friend all those years ago, I never would have known that generosity.

Through the years, I've tried to honor John's generosity by reaching out to people I consider to have high potential and

offering them the benefit of my experience. Not everyone catches on.

Once I offered to take a promising younger colleague to lunch. I scheduled a time, and that other person rescheduled—twice! After the third meeting fell through he

said, 'I know you want to talk about your career, but I've got a lot of client demands right now, so can it wait?' He wasn't getting it. I had no intention of talking about my career—I was interested in talking about his.

You may be shy or uncomfortable reaching out to build relationships with more experienced leaders but make the time —even if it's just to "chew the fat," get to know them and allow them to get to know you.

I encourage everyone to make the time and not to be as dense as I was in recognizing the extension of a mentor's hand. This is where meaningful relationships are built and how you find the allies and advocates who will help you advance your career.

– Steve Astle

Remember that sometimes mentors choose you, not the other way around.

This notion is contrary to most of what you hear about finding mentors. And, while you can ask for someone to be your mentor, it takes commitment on both sides to make that relationship a strong one.

Therein lies the notion that a mentor also picks you.

I've found that some of my mentors were previous bosses—sometimes I directly reported to them, and sometimes they were a skip level or two above. They understood how I worked and knew my strengths and weaknesses.

Over the years, they were able to see me grow and develop in other organizations and still provide me with the "tough love" feedback when I needed it.

> "Never be too reticent to ask for help, especially if you want to emulate someone in a certain way. Ask for an informational interview, and, if you feel like there is a connection to be nurtured, ask that person to be a mentor. And be sure to articulate what you are seeking in that relationship."
>
> – Donna Uchida

Take The First Step

The first step in building beneficial career relationships is to make time for it.

This sounds easy, but it's the one thing most of us don't do when managing our careers. You have to make time to connect with your mentors—to reach up and across the organization and build relationships in every corner.

All the leaders interviewed for this book mentioned this, as well as the importance of making time to develop their own teams and to be a mentor and coach.

> "My philosophy is to have regular feedback sessions with my team, rather than wait for the formal review processes. I meet weekly with direct reports, and the dialogue is honest and open, so they can get better as individuals and our programs can get better."
>
> – Marta Newhart

Be Invested in the Relationship

When finding (or being) a mentor, you also can't be afraid to have the tough conversations. Mentor relationships are only as valuable as you allow them to be.

When that person is someone you trust and is willing to give you both encouragement and a reality check, you will see tangible personal and professional growth.

Every so often, I hear from mentors about their frustrations with the lack of understanding some people have about how to maximize the relationship. One executive told me, "One person I have tried to mentor only comes to me when there is a problem. It's as if they don't want to think for themselves and only call me to solve whatever crisis they are in at the moment."

Like nurturing your network, you must nurture your mentor relationships as well. You can't call upon them only when you need help. You should have a regular cadence of connection.

Maybe it's a quarterly coffee meeting. Maybe you touch base by phone for 15 minutes every month. Have conversations that are focused on maintaining your connection.

And, equally important, be willing to be a resource for your mentors should they need something from you. Share a note, a comment, an article—it can be your favorite BBQ recipe if you know it's something your mentor enjoys.

REAL WORLD LESSONS:
WHY ARE YOU IN THIS BUSINESS?

Mostly what I do for mentoring is have meetings with people. I do formal mentoring and coaching through Page Society and sometimes friends or colleagues have asked me to mentor someone. But it's always informal with me.

The first thing I ask is 'What kind of person do you want to be? What kind of career do you want to have? Why are you in this business?

Recently I was talking to a group of Georgetown graduates. I said to them, 'What do you want and why do you want it? Don't give me the answer you think I want to hear.

Some of you are in it for the money. If that's true, there are certain choices you make and companies you should look at for the money. Some of you want it for the excitement. You want to be next to rock stars or quarter backs. Some of you want interesting experiences around the world, so work for a global company. Some of you are in for work family balance—a job is a means to an end for taking care of your family. Some of you are in it for corporate social responsibility.

There's no wrong answer. But be truthful with yourself about what you want and why you're doing it.

– John Onoda

◀ Remember This!

You don't have to invite someone formally to be a mentor or to be mentored. When you find that trusted source to go to for career conversations, go with it.

If adding formality to the relationship by asking someone to be a mentor suddenly stifles your ability to have meaningful discussions, don't anoint the relationship with the mentor title.

Once you have identified Mentors, Champions and Allies, set a cadence to reach out and stay connected – not just when you need something. Reciprocity is important, so always seek ways to be a resource to others as well.

Nurturing your network never stops. It's an essential part of your job as a leader and cannot be put on the back burner if you want your career to flourish.

CHAPTER 6
Career Derailers and "Aha Moments"

Everyone has a story to tell when they reflect on their career choices.

You head down roads known and unknown. You can find moments that turn into amazing opportunities or missteps.

Whatever career path you follow, it's highly likely you will come face-to-face with potential derailers. A derailer is a challenge that requires improvement if you are to realize your potential.

Everyone has challenges, and everyone can get derailed—no one is immune. There are derailers that you may never choose to improve or master, and yet, to be the best professional you can be, you must address the mindsets and behaviors which get in the way of you moving forward.

Derailers can…

- have the potential to limit your progress

- be linked to a talent that's taken to an extreme

- taint the perspective of others to the point it seems you can do nothing right

- never be compensated for with multiple strengths

Closely linked to derailers are the "aha moments" where you realize what you're doing and how you're thinking just isn't working. These are the lessons that we take with us for life.

From success comes experience and from failure comes wisdom! This chapter shares some insights about what can derail you as a communications professional, as well as some "aha moments" from the executives interviewed for this book.

◄ NOTES FROM ANGEE

Naturally, I have had a few career derailers come to my attention over the years. I've always been enthusiastic about getting things done quickly. I would see the path *so clearly*, I would forget that I needed to bring others along on the journey to ensure success for whatever project or program I was leading.

I had one wise boss who stopped me before I alienated the entire team. He reminded me to get everyone on the same page and delegate to allow my team to learn and grow. Remove roadblocks for them rather than ramming through on my own.

It changed how I led and changed how my team enjoyed the journey. I'm forever grateful for that lesson!

LESSONS LEARNED

"Over aggressiveness. Over competitiveness. Arrogance. These qualities will derail any career.

If you think you're better than everyone in the room, you're in the wrong room. You must listen to ideas from people who are closer, who have better ideas than you. Title is left at the door. Everybody is equal when it comes to ideas on the board.

Whether you've been in this field for two weeks or 10 years, all ideas are good. Go in with that spirit and everyone feels they can contribute."

– David Albritton

"When someone gets stuck in one place, with one company, they don't have the ability to think beyond the boundaries. That can definitely derail them.

I also see communications people get sidetracked by frustration when they try hard to justify programs. Maybe it's something you've created and love, but you have to ask yourself, 'What is this achieving and what am I doing?' Then let it go if it needs to go."

– Cory Curtis

"I ran marketing and communications for one company. I had a reputation for developing campaigns that elevated the brand and contributed to the organization being named to the industry's coveted "Best of" lists. In my mind, I was proactive in securing media coverage that clearly conveyed the company's scientific breakthroughs and achievements.

But my CEO didn't think the organization was getting enough news coverage and routinely asked what I was doing to make it happen. Ultimately, he ended up hiring someone over me – a journalist whose experience included being a producer for a nightly news show. In his view, that gave her credibility.

My after-the-fact "aha moment" was that the CEO was telling me what was important to him, but I was hearing other messages. I was focused on the results, the team's performance, and missed what was most important to him – securing national news coverage. My work was not aligned with his priority.

– Ann Marie Gothard

"Business needs and communications needs are not always perfectly lined up, but comms always has a role in advancing the business—and you can't be derailed thinking otherwise. You have to learn that good enough is sometimes really good, and exactly what is needed, so run with it.

Also, don't get attached to perfection—it's a farce. And taking yourself too seriously will derail you for sure. You need to have a sense of humor, but not be a clown."

– Jason Hunke

"What derails communicators is separating the day from the night. I believe that you have to take your whole self to work every day.

We are not just professional people during the day and emotional people at night. We've all gone through tragedy of one kind or another. For me, it was getting bone cancer in my twenties and having my shoulder and partial right arm replaced.

Going to work and being there for each other, no matter our level, not pretending that things are okay, but acknowledging them as they are, we build stronger teams. Be real. You will gain the trust of your team and your colleagues.

Life happens to everyone, not just those in the trenches. Show empathy to others. Someday you will need it, too.

Traditional ways of thinking will compete with the rest of our daily lives. But integrating work, home and your entire life will make you a more productive leader and a more satisfied person."

— Marta Newhart

"Micromanagement and not doing the highest value of work are huge derailers. At the leadership level, you have to delegate and trust and accept the risk associated with that.

You will be held accountable and take your lumps. Those who don't want to take the risks end up micromanaging all levels down and working themselves into exhaustion. Some people may be B players and not A players, and they can make a whole career because they aren't taking risks. If you want that kind of career, okay. But we're talking about consequential careers—and those require risk taking.

Another form of risk aversion I see is when people won't hire strong staff. Top people have no problem hiring someone stronger than they are. I do that to give you that part of the job you love, so I can focus on things I'm great at doing.

And one more—people not fulfilling their potential often guard their work, or worse, take credit for other's work. That is totally demoralizing to the team, and you will drive away A players."

– John Onoda

"Not using critical thinking is a big derailer. …You have to pause for root causes and identify obstacles. Of course, when you are rushed to make a decision (which is daily), sometimes you forget that pause. Pause, think, plan, and go will enable high support.

Also, the lack of strategic agility—exploring different paths to achieve an outcome. It's easy to fall into rinse-wash-repeat or 'I've been here' attitude. You may have been, but the circumstances are different. The company is not in the exact same place, nor the publics you will be addressing.

Being strategic without the agility piece won't work."

– Krista Todd

"Lack of courage. Lack of standing up for what you know is right. Lack of understanding for the nuances of internal politics. And lack of good cultural fit is often what derails people at the highest level."

– Donna Uchida

◀ Remember This!

The motivational speaker Tony Robbins has often said, "Turn decades into days." He would interview successful people to find out what they did to reach the heights they achieved. He would take those lessons that were accumulated over decades of experiences and apply what he could to his own life.

The insights in this book merely scratch the surface. As you have networking conversations with peers, mentors and other leaders, be curious about what lessons they may have learned the hard way. It makes for some interesting and insightful conversation. When enough time has passed, we can laugh at ourselves and our mistakes.

CHAPTER 7
But Wait... I Think I Want To Go Out On My Own!

Over the course of your career, there may come a time—by choice or by chance—that you consider going out on your own. This can be a career move filled with risks and rewards, and it's definitely worth talking about.

I decided to include this chapter in the middle of the book because that's where this decision often shows up—towards the middle of a career. And when it shows up, it can often throw you for a loop, just like a stick getting caught in the spokes of your bicycle when you were a kid.

When I've spoken to communications leaders who have deliberately gone out on their own at some stage in their career, there have been a few common themes:

- *The desire for a more flexible work schedule* – essential because of various life events
- *The urge to be an entrepreneur* – own your own company and build it
- *The planets aligned* – enough former colleagues or executives

asked you to do it, so you felt like it was an opportunity you had to explore

And then there are those who stumbled into communications consulting. Someone may become an "accidental consultant" because a corporate restructuring eliminated their position, so this might be a good interim income opportunity while looking for a new position.

Alternatively, it may just seem like as good a time as any, given whatever market trends make getting a full-time position more difficult.

Regardless of why you find yourself on your own, there are a few things I've learned from talking and working with as well as a few tidbits from my own move.

Getting Started

Whether this is going to be a short-term or long-term opportunity for you, having your goals laid out before you launch is essential. Having clear short- and long-term goals will be the cornerstone to determining what types of clients you want to attract.

If you are filling the gaps while looking for a new role, you may want only short-term project work. If this is going to be a sustainable, long-term business, you may target more strategic opportunities or gigs that may even bring you in-house for interim periods of time.

Like any business with a plan, it all starts with your value proposition.

If you're reading this book, I'm going to assume you are a communications professional, so you already have a specific skill set that you are marketing to your prospective clients. But communications is a broad field, and you likely have some areas of expertise you would rather hone in on, so that you are doing work where you can immediately provide value.

It's important to get clear on what you have to offer and what your differentiators are. Make yourself your own client and create a communications strategy to tell your story in a way that others will quickly understand what you have to offer.

Your personal communications strategy should have three components:

- *Your positioning statement* – This answers the question, "tell me a little about you" or "what do you do?" Some people think of this as an elevator pitch, but I encourage you to think more conversationally when creating this message.

  Be clear and concise. Imagine a picture frame that allows the listener to understand who you are, not only from where you've been but also with intention regarding where you are going.

  For example: *"I am a communications leader who helps late-stage start-ups tell their story to key stakeholders, investors and employees."*

- *Your "why" statement* – Why do you do this work? Why are you making a change from whatever you were doing before? Why do you want to work with the person you're talking to? It all starts with why.

- *Your professional objective* – What do you want to do next? Be clear if you are a consultant seeking new projects and describe the type of client you enjoy working with, the type of work you want to do.

If you are transitioning, don't be afraid to be clear that you are in a job search but taking on consulting projects in the interim. Others can help you if they understand your true goals.

Targeting Potential Clients

Once you have your personal communication strategy down, you will want to research your target market and determine the clients you want to work with.

This is where growing your network will be essential. Chances are, you will attract clients who have worked with you in the past and know what you can do for them.

Don't be afraid to connect with as many people as possible— simply let them know what you are up to so that you are on their radar should they need a helping hand.

I know, this sounds easier than it is in reality. After all, this is all about N-E-T-W-O-R-K-I-N-G, a term that is loathed and an activity that is often seen as painful!

Try breaking it down in these easier to digest steps:

- **_Start with your close-in network._** Think about those people you've worked with and for in the last five or even 10 years. Hopefully, you've stayed in touch reasonably well over the years (see chapter 5). Reach out with a friendly hello and state your interest in scheduling a call, coffee or lunch meeting to catch up.

  Important note: These reconnection calls must be genuine and not just about what you need from the other person. Use this opportunity to come into the conversation with authentic curiosity about what's happening in their world, how you can be a resource for them and share what you're doing and how they may be able to help you with appropriate introductions.

- ***Bring ideas to the table about the kind of work you want to do and the kind of clients you want***. Literally write down those industries and company names. Use that document as a brainstorming tool to see if your close-in network connections can help you come up with ideas that you may have overlooked

  Then start talking about who that person knows who you should know. Would they be willing to do an introduction?

  This is a great time to offer sending a paragraph that they could easily edit or forward when making an email introduction on your behalf. Make it easy for them, and you are more likely to expand your network quickly.

- ***Always follow up with a thank-you note***. And extend your thank-you after you've acted on their introduction.

  For example, if Sherry introduces you to Jim, after your meeting with Jim, send Sherry another note letting her know that your meeting went well and you are happy to have met through her kind introduction.

  People like to know that they've helped—and it makes them more likely to do it again when appreciated.

The Pricing Puzzle

Determining your pricing can be tricky, and it's another place you want to do your homework. You've likely hired plenty of consultants, so you have an idea of what the market bears in your industry or geographic region; however, when it comes to determining your own value, it's common to price yourself too low just to get the business.

If you are uncertain, reach out to your network (either consultants or leaders who hire them) and be willing to reciprocate. I have found most people to be generous with information when there is professional trust and respect.

The partnerships, referrals and general support that come from these conversations tend to make a significant and positive difference for those who have taken the consulting path.

The one biggest piece of advice I have when it comes to pricing is to be confident and unapologetic in the numbers you set. If you're too high, you'll know soon enough. If you are too low, you may not be perceived as the expert and others will get the gig.

No matter where you fall in the rate scale, be able to articulate the value you bring, and why you're worth every penny.

Getting The Business And Doing The Business

In my interviews, I often find people looking to return to an in-house role after being on their own simply want to get back to doing the work, rather than getting the work.

It makes sense. After all, you love being a communications professional, not necessarily being a sales person.

If you aren't someone who loves to develop the business, one of your biggest challenges will be continuing to keep the pipeline of future clients full while delivering quality work. It can be a juggling act because, when you are busy on client work, you may not be having those networking conversations to get more work in the weeks and months ahead.

It's easy to put off those "future business" conversations because you're too busy right now to take on something new. But, prospective clients often require weeks or months to turn into a contract of any sort.

I know from my own experience that waiting for a lull in work is too late, so dedicate time even when you're busy to keep up your new business conversations. Ongoing relationship building is a top priority when you're out on your own.

Whether you have long-term clients who keep you fully engaged or short-term clients with intermittent projects, knowing yourself and knowing if you are willing and able to spend the time getting or doing the business will determine if being on your own is for now or forever for your career.

Some people are very fortunate to have a cornerstone client who has kept them gainfully employed for years.

One communications leader I spoke with recently had 10 years of following a team of executives who were serial entrepreneurs. She met them when working in-house as their head of communications.

Once that company was purchased, this team went on to create a series of new successful businesses and with each one, asked her to join them. This went on for multiple start-ups that were each acquired successfully.

This scenario worked out extremely well for a few years, until that team of executives decided to enjoy their good fortune and take a break from starting another new company. That's when she had to make a decision on her next career chapter.

Should she continue as a consultant, having to essentially start from scratch on identifying new clients? Or was it time to go back in-house and be a full-time employee?

For this leader, she opted to build new clients and continue to consult. But it was a tough decision for her. If you find yourself at a crossroads like this, the most important thing is to know what is most important to you at this time of your life.

Priorities change. Our needs and wants evolve.

Risks and Rewards

There are always a few surprises that come up for people when they ebb and flow between being a consultant and being employed by an organization. These surprises can be good or bad; I simply refer to them as "the risks and rewards" of consulting.

Here are a few I've heard consistently:

- "I can pick and choose the work that I do."
- "Consulting provided me with the flexibility I really needed at the time."
- "I really miss working with a team."
- "Working from home has proven harder than expected."
- "I prefer to be able to see a project or program through from beginning to end."

"I can pick and choose the work that I do."

As a consultant, you can choose your clients.

You don't have to do those extra assignments that have nothing to do with the communications strategy you need to implement. You can work with organizations that represent products or services you believe in. You can say "no" to the abusive executive.

Going to work every day can be incredibly rewarding because you get to do work you enjoy.

"Consulting provided me with the flexibility I really needed at the time."

Whether it's a growing family, caring for an aging parent, dealing with a major move, or any number of life's challenges that sometimes require us to just take a break from 60+ hour work weeks, consulting can be a great approach to taking on the amount of work that you can do well given your current circumstances.

Just remember that circumstances change, so understanding how to move from increased or decreased responsibility is important to consider as you create your long view of your consulting goals.

"I really miss working with a team."

When you are accustomed to working with a team of people, you may take for granted that there is a group of built-in collaborators for literally every project you tackle.

Whether you walk down the hall and share ideas with someone in another department or connect on a global conference call with the entire communications function, you are all focused on the same over-arching business goals of the organization.

"Working from home has proven harder than expected."

Even in today's era of working remotely, when you don't have that tether to the corporate office, working from home sometimes is just a little more distracting than expected.

Whether you create a home office that can be in a less distracting part of the house, or you take up part-time or full-time residence in a shared office space like "WeWork," find the solution that allows you to feel connected to others while getting the space to do the work.

"I prefer to be able to see a project or program through from beginning to end."

So often consultants are hired for a piece of the work, rather than the project from inception to completion. For more senior level communications professionals, not being included in the strategy portion of the work can be frustrating. Similarly, not seeing the results of your work can be unsatisfying.

Consulting often means being brought in for the extra workload, handling a crisis where no one has your expertise or simply providing good advice that may or may not be implemented. It's normal to have mixed feelings about being only part of a program vs. leading it from soup to nuts.

Just be sure to check in with yourself to understand what is most important in how you work so that you can successfully maneuver through your career.

Transitioning Back To Being An Employee

If you decide to move back into a full-time role after being a consultant, it's time to revisit that personal communications strategy described earlier in this chapter. This time, your messages will be slightly different because you will be designing it to fit the new direction of becoming an employee.

To reiterate the three key messages mentioned earlier:

- Your positioning statement, answering the question what do you do?
- Your "why" statement, answering why do you want to go back in-house?
- Your professional objective, answering what do you want to do next?

This isn't complicated (though we all tend to make it much more so than it is). Compared to how you positioned yourself as a consultant, you will pivot to making a move toward being an employee. Change the words, and you change the results.

Strut Your Stuff

Once you get past the basics of these three key messages, you should be ready to share examples of the types of projects and clients you have worked with over the time of your consulting. Even if it's only been a few small projects, include details of the value you brought to the client and the results achieved because of your contribution.

There is a reasonable expectation from employers that, if you are simply filling the income gap while looking for a new role, you won't have huge programs as examples.

However, if your gap consists of only a couple of small projects over a period that is months or even years, you will also need to illustrate how you are staying current with current communications skills.

In recent years, there have been so many technology advancements and changes to how audiences receive their messages (and the pace in which they receive them), you will likely get questions regarding what efforts you took to keep up. This is where certificate programs or even just a few classes on the latest communications technologies could be beneficial.

Also, in my work with corporate clients who are seeking communications leaders, I have learned they prefer to include consultants in the candidate line up with relevant in-house experience at some reasonably recent point in their career. I sometimes get pushback if the candidate has worked on his/her own for decades and suddenly is seeking a senior-level corporate communications leadership role.

Hiring Leader Concerns

Through the years, hiring leaders have shared with me some concerns about people moving back into a corporate role after being on their own. Being able to overcome these objections is another important part of your communication strategy:

"Does this person really want to report to someone after being their own boss for so long?"

This is such a subjective question that you can only do your best to demonstrate how you've always worked well with leadership, structure and expectations. When you've been "the decider" in your own business for any length of time, it's sometimes hard to give up that role and go back to being an employee.

Your ability to describe how you can manage up, down and across an organization will determine your success. How have you done it before? One way to demonstrate this is to give solid examples as an employee and how you retained long-term clients with this skill.

"Can this person navigate office politics?"

Being a consultant certainly doesn't mean you are immune to corporate politics of your clients, but it does mean that the day-to-day politics were likely not part of your overall management requirements.

My first thought is to check in with yourself to know if office politics is something you manage well. I speak from personal experience in saying that sometimes you have to get real with yourself and know your strengths. If office politics is a failing, can you endure them, or do they drive you to distraction?

Knowing the answer in your heart will help you answer honestly when the question comes up. If you know that office politics are something you manage well, you will be able to once again give examples of real situations where being politically astute enhanced your success.

"Can this person manage projects and programs from beginning to end, rather than just pieces of it?"

Once again, linking back to stories of when you've done it before will help illustrate your capabilities to anyone seeking to hire you into their organization. Often people who were "embedded" with a project or program can more easily demonstrate how they manage the full scope of work.

Speak in specifics, rather than anecdotal or hypothetical. Be industry-specific if you can. When sharing examples, set the scene—what did you do and how did it turn out? Focus on results and how you added value to the organization.

After You're Hired

Once you land in your new full-time role, it's up to you to build those internal relationships quickly to illustrate that you are a valuable member of the team. People have assumptions about consultants. Prove them wrong.

One effective way to get started on the right foot from the beginning is to create a 90-day plan for yourself. A great resource for making any job change is the book *The First 90 Days* by Michael D. Watkins.[1] Some examples of what to do include:

- *Knowledge & Skills:* Discover what you most need to learn, from whom, and how you can learn it. Focus on the right mix of technical, cultural and political learning.

- *Culture:* Discover, understand, and begin to adapt to the culture — the attitudes, behaviors, values and processes that lead to decisions.

- *Clarity:* Understand the mission and vision for your team and your role within it. If it's in leading the team, develop and communicate a compelling mission and vision for what the team will become. Outline clear and easy-to-understand tactics for getting there.

- *Priorities:* Identify key goals and pursue them relentlessly.

- *Leadership:* For your team, define assessment criteria and evaluate the team you inherited. Move deftly to make necessary changes. Find the optimal balance between developing existing talent, bringing in individuals from the outside, and promoting high-potential team members.

  Beyond your team, get to know the leadership of the company. Start with your immediate manager and his/

her peers. Introduce yourself. Understand their drivers and constraints. Continue meeting and learning about leaders across the organization and up the hierarchy.

- ***Organization:*** As the leader of a team, identify the most important supporting changes you need to make in the talent, structure, and processes of the organization. Put a plan in place for addressing the most pressing organizational challenges.

  As a team member, understand the structure and processes within the organization. Build relationships across functions to understand how things get done.

- ***Alliances:*** Build personal credibility and create key alliances. Understand who has influence and power.

- ***Early Wins:*** Organize the right set of initiatives to secure early wins. Show continual and demonstrable progress.

Being deliberate and planning that first 90 days will help positively set your entire tenure at any organization. It also applies to when you get promoted within your current company, which is what we will talk about next.

◀ Remember This!

Many people want to stretch their entrepreneurial wings and go out on their own. Whether by chance or choice, be planful in your decision to make the leap to self-employment. The more prepared you are, the more likely you will succeed.

If it turns out, you want or need to go back to being an employee, hang your hat on the fact that you had the courage to make the leap and take note of what you learned and accomplished. Those lessons can only help you in your next role.

CHAPTER 8
Congratulations on Your Promotion!

You've been doing all the right things. You've become a strategic communications leader who is respected throughout your organization. You have a seat at the leadership table, and you are bringing value to your organization and developing your team.

Chances are you have been practicing the best leadership qualities required to be successful in your new role. But what are some things you should do and some you should stop doing when you make the leap to the executive suite?

When I have the opportunity to help a company hire a new executive to lead communications, I always encourage the candidate to create a 90-day plan, similar to what was mentioned in Chapter 7. That plan is not only about the work they will be doing but also those things that just get you on good footing with your new team and your fellow executives.

A few things that I recommend include:

- Communications is more than just a function. Your ability to communicate well with your new team will determine your success.

Sit down as a group and individually to get to know the team and have an idea of their skills and ability to function in the organization as you hope to lead it. Let them get to know you as well.

- Building relationships with the team quickly will help the transition be smoother for all of you.

  Give yourself and the team time for a fair evaluation of the skills they have and the skills you need to move the organization forward based on the priorities of the organization. You may have to make some changes, but you may have people just in the wrong seat. Your coaching might be all that is necessary.

- If you do need to make changes, communicate clearly regarding the needs of the organization so that those who can will step up. And those who can't will know why they may need to find opportunities elsewhere.

- If you're being promoted from within, it's tough to go from peer (and often friend) to boss. The relationship will change, and it won't be easy for anyone.

  Have a candid conversation with those you now have to lead so that you understand where boundaries may have to be created. If others on the team feel there is favoritism because of friendships, there will challenges ahead.

- It's easy to make assumptions and take the word of one person's opinion on how communications ran before you got there. While it's good to take in the opinions of others, it's important to seek evidence to form your own conclusions.

- Truly learning the culture takes time. Everyone wants to jump in and have impact quickly—it's totally understandable. But if you step on toes because you don't understand the culture, you can be derailed before you have a chance to shine.

Take advantage of those first weeks and really get immersed on "who's who" in the organization. Influencers are not always the ones with the biggest titles.

One on one meetings with various functional leads and influencers will help you navigate the culture more quickly.

This chapter is the communications equivalent of convenience shopping—it's the one spot in the book where everyone interviewed, myself included, had the opportunity to weigh in with a list of do's and don'ts.

You can scan the information quickly and file away the bits that speak to you the most.

DO THIS!

- Immediately start thinking and acting more like a business partner well beyond your functional expertise. Figure out how your function contributes to how the company makes money and make future functional decisions based on that impact.

- You're now part of the executive team, you should try to get a better understanding of how other executives view your function's contributions to their success and that of the company, so you can make strategy, personnel and budgeting decisions based on that feedback.

- One of the most important things you can do for the company is to start thinking about who your successor is and help to grow that person enough to fill your executive chair at some point in the future.

– David Albritton

Behave as though you're always being watched, because you are. People scrutinize leaders, sometimes critically—it comes with the territory—but more often with admiration.

So, give them something to really admire—not just intelligence or shrewdness (which are more abundant than we'd like to think), but kindness, moral courage or good humor (which are more rare than we'd like to think).

– Steve Astle

Ask questions and learn from those who have been there longer. Find a mentor on the executive team (ideally from outside of your line of business—if you're in comms, consider the CFO, etc), and commit to meeting with them one-to-two times a month outside of regular business meetings. And always be curious.

– Cory Curtis

- Know thyself—invest the time to develop your intellectual, social, and political confidence.

- Project an executive presence at all times in formal and informal settings—evolve your professional identity.

- Build supportive relationships—a core network of people you can turn to for advice, encouragement, and mentorship.

- Set boundaries—be responsive yet have the strength to unplug and recharge as needed.

- Immediately assess talent and develop bench strength—with personal attention diverted to larger, organizational issues. It's important to have someone on the team that can ensure operations are running smoothly.

- Check your fears at the door—trust your judgment and listen to your instincts.

- Be a visible leader—each day strive to have at least one meaningful touchpoint or interaction with direct reports and team members.

- Have fun and bring a level of enthusiasm to work every day—projecting positive energy will result in high-levels of engagement and motivate the team to perform to the best of their abilities.

– Ann Marie Gothard

- Focus more on being a leader than a manager.

- Forge strategic alliances with other members of the executive team, so that your people can effectively address the most important challenges facing the organization (because work of this importance ALWAYS requires strategic partnerships with other parts of the enterprise).

- Be a champion and advocate for your function in every key discussion.

– John Onoda

- Remember managing up is just as important as managing down or sideways. How you engage your CEO (or other executives you work with) is critically important and a different skill than managing who reports to you or your direct boss. Both are critical skills.

- Build a strong connection with the finance team, the legal team and the IT team. They may not seem core to your work, but you will need their help one day and they are important allies. Mutual trust and respect with other business functions is critical.

- Move from sharing information to making recommendations and problem solving. It's fine to ask for help at the executive level but always start with your recommended solution, not just sharing the problem. Teams expect their leader to have a POV on what needs to happen.

- Know the business, not just the communications issue(s). As an executive level communications pro, you need to grasp the broader business, finance, legal, regulatory and marketing aspects of whatever industry you are in. Be an expert at communications, and know in general terms your industry, how it measures success, who are your competitors, and how it all works.

- Dress the part. This sounds obvious but the adage of dressing for the job you want, not just the job you have, is worth remembering. Impressions matter and the stories people tell is the business we are in as communicators. The story people tell about you will be informed by the first impressions of your appearance.

- Be a voracious reader. It makes your thinking and your writing better.

– Jason Hunke

- Keep learning.

- Mentor others.

- Always be respectful.

- Be accountable.

– Michelle Jones

- Leaders at this level need to start taking a bird's eye view. Look at the big picture. Look at your teams and organization as an integrated whole, not the sum of its parts. Understand how all the pieces come together.

  If you grew up in a marketing organization, for example, look beyond a consumer approach and take a company approach. This is probably the biggest mind shift for new leaders. This is the time to end any biases.

- To succeed at this level, you need to understand context. How does your company make money, what are the market and customer trends? How do you compete and win?

  Understand the inside too. What is happening with the internal culture? What is the culture you are trying to drive? And what do you want that to translate into as your company purpose?

- Ask for feedback, listen and act upon the feedback. Be open to change because you will win and so will your company.

  – Marta Newhart

- Start with an audit—internal and external with key stakeholders. Find the 'perception' gaps and build that as part of your strategy.

- Asking others what they need more of when you are in communications opens up a lot of conversation and opportunity. Don't make assumptions early—gather data.

- Remember yours is a tough role, but you were

promoted into it because you can handle it. Keep that confidence.

- There will be challengers and people who may doubt you or your strategy. This is normal, and you should push through. People may remember you in that 'almost executive' role, not executive.

- Reset their perception. Set a vision, build a great team, deliver results and show value.

– Krista Todd

- Approach most opportunities as a business person, with a specialty in communications rather than as a communications person.

- Understand the broader business—even if it means some online financials classes and understanding a financial statement.

- You are at the table because you have proven yourself, so be an equal, relevant part of any executive conversation.

- Continue to be a team leader as well as a member of the team in any opportunity and demonstrate ethics and decisions that will reinforce your reputation.

– Donna Uchida

STOP DOING THIS!

Assuming that as you've taken on the new role as a senior executive you now have a larger team and a larger set of responsibilities, you will need to stop believing that you can be on top and aware of EVERY issue that happens within your organization.

Corporations are huge, complex entities with a wide variety of things happening every day and it's physically and mentally impossible to absorb and manage it all.

Train and work with your team to understand what the most critical issues are that you need and want to be aware of and be part of the decision chain, but outside of that, empower and trust your team to handle the rest of it.

– David Albritton

Participating in gossip. Gossiping is never a good idea, but if you've gotten this far in your career and still tolerate gossip, knock it off immediately. I'm embarrassed to admit that I can still be seduced by gossip myself, despite my acute awareness of gossip's corrosiveness.

Great leaders stop gossip in its tracks, and the rest of us should follow their example.

– Steve Astle

- Stop micro-managing. At the executive table you need time and capacity to focus on the work ahead, not the work to be done. Be certain that your team(s) are well-equipped to make decisions, move ahead and be successful without you being an impediment.

- Stop bad management behaviors. If you don't know what yours are, take a self-assessment profile or engage with a coach. At the executive table you both represent the business and also model behavior for how employees show up in the workplace and in the community on your company's behalf. Lead with integrity.

- Stop talking about how you did things at your last job. You're not there anymore.

– Cory Curtis

- Acting like an individual contributor

- Attending every meeting—delegate and allow others the chance to learn and grow

- The thinking of others—figuring things out and giving the answers to their questions

- Focusing only on the goals of your department— expand your horizons and look daily at the big picture

- Recalling the "good old days" and citing too frequently how you've done things in the past

- Being the designated meeting scribe or note-taker (specific to women)

– Ann Marie Gothard

- Don't allow other departments (especially legal and finance) or business units position you as a "second-class citizen" when key decisions are being debated

- Don't feel you must micro-manage and know everything your staff is doing because you are afraid of being perceived as uninformed when asked a question by a C-suite exec.

- Don't work on matters that can be delegated to talented lieutenants. Let go of everything except those things that only you can do.

  – John Onoda

- Don't take things personally. You better have thick skin as you move up the ranks in any business and in any organization. Politics and relationships will always be a factor in your work and realizing that business comes before personal is key.

- Don't worry about trying to be friends with everyone. Personal relationships matter but don't expect, or desire, to be friends with those you manage, your peer group, or your leader. You can build meaningful relationships built on respect, trust, reciprocity, and mutual admiration.

- A great working relationship is more important than being friends outside the office, and the more senior you get the lonelier you may feel. Leading is not the same as socializing or people-pleasing.

- At the same time, don't be an asshole. Relationships matter and it's free to be nice.

- Don't write long emails or memos. Being pithy matters. And it's really hard. Practice it.

- Don't suck all the oxygen out of the room. Talk less and listen more. You'll learn something, and people may just surprise you with their perspective, intelligence and abilities if you give them some space. Make room for everyone to be at the table. Inclusion matters and drives results and innovation.

– Jason Hunke

- Don't do your old job—start delegating.

- Stop looking at your work e-mail the second you wake up.

- Stop looking at your work e-mail until the second you go to sleep.

– Michelle Jones

- Don't spread yourself too thin. Focus and spend your time on the things that matter to you. Not the things that just come your way. That's a defensive approach to your career.

- An offensive approach is when you are in charge of where and when you spend your time. By the way, your team will be watching. They will spend their time there, too. So choose wisely.

- Don't be afraid to disappoint people, especially if you think what you are doing will benefit the organization.

– Marta Newhart

- Stop acting as an individual contributor or manager—your responsibility is now to lead. It will be tough to let go of some of the work you love, that is familiar, that you know you can nail...but your mindset and leadership needs to change just as your role has changed.

- Don't worry about 'small' challenges or problems. They will come everyday, so there's no need to think about it more than necessary. Learn from everything and move on.

– Krista Todd

- Stop looking at organizational issues from your communications lens—you need to offer the broader business lens.

- Be solutions-oriented—stop raising challenges without having a way to overcome the obstacle.

– Donna Uchida

Remember This!

Marshall Goldsmith tells it best in his book, *What Got You Here Won't Get you There* (The title alone says *so much!*). In it, he describes executives who have risen to the top ranks of their organizations. But many of the skills and habits that helped them achieve those heights may not be the ones to take them further.

Take a hard look at what you did to get you that promotion, but don't be blind to the behaviors that need to change now that you're there. The sage advice from those interviewed here is a great place to start.

CHAPTER 9
Words Of Wisdom

We all walk through our careers being given advice—sometimes good and sometimes not so helpful. As we reflect back, there is always a morsel or two that made a difference in our careers.

I've been incredibly fortunate to have so many mentors and champions along the way in my career—there are not enough pages to write all the great advice I've received! But one that keeps coming back to me is, "The answer is always 'no' if you don't ask the question."

From a career standpoint, these are important words whether you're talking about career goals with your boss or looking to land that new client. From a personal standpoint, simply asking could change the course of your life.

This chapter shares a sampling of the best career advice received by the professionals I interviewed for this book. It is my hope, and theirs, too, that these lifetimes of experience will help you avoid some pitfalls on your own career path.

"Working for Sears, Roebuck and Co. after getting out of the Navy had a profound impact on me. The Senior Vice President of Communications at the time was Ron Culp. He gave me many words of wisdom those years he worked there, but the best advice was, 'be strategic.' It changed how I did that job because of those simple words.

In this context, Ron's use of the word 'strategic' took on a couple of meanings for me. One meaning was, "Don't just think about your next job and the job after that—think about what you're learning, exposed to, influencing, responsible for in this job and make sure it makes you qualified for future opportunities with increased responsibilities."

Another was, "Anybody can write a press release about the latest product or service or issue within any company. Be the person that does the work to fully understand the business objectives and the value proposition of the new offering or latest company decision, so that the story you tell on behalf of the company fully resonates with every key internal and external stakeholder audience'."

– David Albritton

"I was one of several people assigned to work with a psychologist who was brought in to help manage a problem executive – someone who was senior to us. At the end of the process, we were wrapping up and I asked the consultant – almost as an afterthought – if he had any advice for me.

'Lose the nice thing,' the consultant told me. 'Why do you have to be so nice? It's not always effective.'

He then told me that I should set a personal goal. 'In the

next three months, I want you to leave at least one meeting and have someone say about you under their breath, 'What an asshole!' You'll never be a real asshole—you're too nice a guy—but you'd benefit by sliding down the curve a bit.'

Unconsciously, I wanted to be liked. Sometimes tough decisions don't make you popular—but good leadership isn't about popularity."

– Steve Astle

"Composer John Cage has a philosophy of 'Start anywhere.' Often we have paralysis. We think whatever we're doing has to be perfect. We ponder, where do I start?

When you have that big hairy audacious thing, start anywhere to get there.

Iteration is a good thing. You don't know the answer or the outcome. We always are driven for outcome and have little room for failure.

But nothing cool will happen without a little failure, so start anywhere!"

– Cory Curtis

"I was very naïve about corporate politics for a very long time. Not just once. I finally had a mentor who was straightforward about this. You have to develop political chops if you want to survive. I always ran from that because it sounded so negative.

I learned that politics is not about being a jerk—it is about understanding other people's motives and agendas, then being creative to align with your own and get things done."

– Jason Hunke

"Always have the courage to present your ideas and opinions. When young in your career, you don't have the confidence and believe you need all the facts to make a contribution.

I remember a moment when I realized exactly what my mentor meant when she said, 'Find your voice.' For me, having a voice speaks to who I am and supports whatever role I have. This is essential when driving communications and leadership."

– Ann Marie Gothard

"My first official communications role was actually leading the function—just when our company was going through major growth and a significant rebranding project. Everything I was about to do, I had never done before.

My boss sat me down and said, 'You have a good reputation, but we're going to invest a lot of money in the company and in this branding initiative because it's important. And you don't know what you're doing. But we're going to get you some help.'

They brought in a consultant to help me, and the project was tremendously successful. My advice is to take risks and don't be afraid of getting help or asking for help. Being out of your comfort zone can be a wonderful thing."

– Michelle Jones

REAL WORLD LESSONS:
DIFFERENT SIDE-STEPS TO SUCCESS

My Mexican mother told me to dare to be different. She would say, "You are different, you look different than the other kids, and you need to accept that and be bold with it because people will criticize you.'"

My family was the only Hispanic family at my school, so, I took her mother's advice to heart and embraced my differences.

"In my 20s and most of my 30s, I was impatient. You could say I was impatient for 20 years. I wanted each career move to be a step up. And when it wasn't, I felt as if I failed.

But it's really true what they say—the side steps are often the most instructive in your career.

I learned the hard way that having a lot of drive and ambition is not as beneficial as it should have been. When I went from working in Asia/Pacific sales to communications, it was a side step, not a level up. Then when I went from Asia/Pacific communications to global communications, it was another side step.

I built on the attributes I had, and it better prepared me for the next role, which was an executive director. Had I not made those side steps, I would have not been able to do the more senior role—I wouldn't have been well-rounded.

That is a lesson that is hard to tell someone in their 20s who just wants to move up the ladder. But it was the smartest thing I did.

People ask, "Why are you taking that job, when it's not a move up?" You have to deal with the peer pressure because they will see it as a demotion, but it's really preparing you for the promotion.

Peer pressure can be a career derailer if you succumb to it. These are important people in your day-to-day life. You spend more time with them than your family. They influence you. You get into this 'group think.' It takes a strong high potential leader to cut through that.

Expectations are the worst things you can carry. They're heavy. They don't do anything for you. The key is to live without expectations, and to help people without needing anything in return. No ulterior motive. No agenda. Just trust that if you are good to others, the good will come back to you."

My mother passed away many years ago from ovarian cancer, so she never saw the full success of my career. But I know she would have delighted in telling all her friends that her little farm girl was able to break through the glass ceiling in corporate America to become the highest-ranking Latina at two Fortune 100 companies!

--Marta Newhart

"The best advice I've received was from my mentor, Al Geduldig, who told me that, among corporate communications professionals, you are either a priest or a warrior.

Priests are like cheerleaders, making a lot of noise but staying safely on the sidelines. Warriors are on the field. They get hit and knocked down a lot, but they are also the ones who score the points. In most organizations, warriors get respect and therefore have a say in important matters. Beyond the obvious, what Al was talking about was the way you handle yourself as an executive. You can play it safe by working in ways in which you avoid accountability (which is pretty easy when you're in a staff function), or you can work in a way in which if something fails, you will be among the accountable (which is what happens with people who have profit-and-loss responsibilities). These are the warriors.

My observation is that the men and women at the top of the communications profession, the ones known for their integrity, leadership and influence, are all warriors at heart."

– John Onoda

"I live by the philosophy that was shared with me years ago—'Say yes to more things than not.'

Even if you have no idea how to do them, you will figure it out. If you keep asking for more and taking on more, the rest will fall into place."

– Krista Todd

"My best advice came from John Onoda. He told me, as I was working in my job, to give up 20-25% of my current responsibilities each year to and take on new work.

Within four to five years, I had a new job because I had created new work. Doing this has allowed me to make a powerful impact at Kaiser Permanente over time."

– Donna Uchida

◀ Remember This!

The first time you land in the executive suite, you will learn many lessons—some due to great leaders who guide you, and some from learning the hard way.

Every new role you take will require you to learn that organization's culture, priorities, business goals and most importantly, the people. Always use that first 90 days to be a sponge by listening and learning.

The more effectively you manage the transition through great planning and immersion, the more successful you will be.

CONCLUSION

As you read the pages of this book, I'm guessing there were a lot of things you already knew but haven't been putting them into action. It's so common for people to put their own career development on the back burner, leaving it to chance that your boss will "take care of you" if you just work hard and do a good job.

Daring to be Deliberate means that you are willing to make time for those things that require, well, *time*.

It includes creating a career action plan which has activities that you will commit to doing monthly, quarterly and annually in support of your career growth and development.

How often will you reach out to people in your network when you don't need their help? For those who you value most, a quick note or coffee meeting should be a regular occurrence.

For those allies you don't want to lose touch with, be willing to be a resource when you hear from them and initiate contact with positive words of encouragement and congratulations whenever possible.

It's easy to forget, or put off making those regular connections, but if you block time—even if it's just one Friday afternoon per month—to do *something* in support of nurturing your network, you are ahead of most people.

Quarterly, take a look at what professional events you can attend or what skills you need to make more of an effort to enhance. Maybe a class, workshop or conference is in order.

Annually, you should take a few hours to reflect on your year and your professional goals. Did you achieve them? How have your values and vision changed because of life changes and priority shifts?

Nothing has to be set in stone, but by taking a moment to check in with yourself, you can adjust your vision and watch it come into view.

Having strong strategic communications leadership is essential for organizations to achieve their goals, maintain a positive reputation and reduce risk. You can be the one to make a difference for many.

And finally, thank you for Daring to be Deliberate! It takes courage to get control of your own career and pay attention to the career goals of those who you can influence through your leadership.

If this book has resonated with you and you're ready to level up your communications career, we should meet. You can find me at ***www.linseycareers.com*** and ***www.daretobedeliberate.com*** to learn more about how we can connect.

CREATING YOUR CAREER VISION

This exercise will help you get clear about what matters most in your life right now. You will find out those things that are absolute deal breakers (or deal makers) when it comes to aligning your values with that of the job you hold.

What comes to you through this vision will begin to come to you in real life. This is about the power of intention, the law of attraction. What you think about is what comes into view.

EXERCISE

Imagine you are in your ideal role – what does it look and feel like?

Reflect on your **values**. Think about what **motivates** you. Consider your **preferences**.

As you begin to write your vision, think about how you can make memorable phrases or sentences to help you articulate the meaning behind each thought. It gives you the opportunity to make the vision more emotional and alive.

Here are a few tips and guidelines for crafting your vision statements by combining your values, motivators and preferences:

- **Use inspiring words.** Our brains are quick to delete or ignore the mundane and commonplace.

- **Mine for words that evoke and trigger** *emotional responses.* They will be more meaningful and memorable.

- **Play to your strengths** in crafting your vision. (I recommend taking the Strengths Finder assessment.[1])

- **Make your vision statements rich and meaningful** to you so they inspire you to uphold them.

Write in positive, present tense as if it is already happening in your life (I am, I have, I do). If you find yourself writing DON'T, NOT, NO—think of the opposite.

EXAMPLES

Health
I am physically active and feel strong and vibrant.

Community
I am working with really smart people who challenge me to be my best.

Environment
My office has a lot of windows and natural light streaming in.

Motivation
I am an expert in my field.
I am in an organization that values my contributions.

Lifestyle
My commute is less than 20 minutes each way.
I have flexibility to work from home a few days per week.

Brainstorming Help

The questions below are simply to get you thinking of multiple aspects that are important considerations at work.

You may have multiple answers to one question, or no answers at all. Be as detailed as you can without assigning a specific job title or career path.

The end result will not be an obvious, "Oh! I should go get (fill in blank with a job title or company name) job." Rather, it may help you identify and articulate the things that are important to you as you have career conversations and create your career action plan.

20 QUESTIONS
When imagining the absolute ideal work situation...

1. What kind of people are your colleagues?

2. What kind of people are your customers or clients? (Old? Young? Motivated? Distressed? Hopeless? Happy?)

3. What type of physical environment do you work in daily?

4. What is the culture of this ideal place?

5. Who is the boss? Where do you fall in the hierarchy?

6. How much flexibility do you have? Describe what flexibility means through your sentences.

7. What are your working hours? How much time do you spend thinking about work when you're not on the job?

8. How much time off do you have?

9. How do you feel when you head to work?

10. How do you feel at the end of each day or week?

11. What gives you satisfaction in this job?

12. How do you know you are being successful in the role?

13. How much money are you making?

14. How does your family perceive this career choice?

15. How do others perceive this career choice?

16. What does your community look like in this role? (example: your community may be your local city; or it may be group of people that expand beyond local, such as veterans or students; or it may be an industry community such as global health nonprofit workers)

17. Where is your place in this community? (Leader, participant, etc.)

18. What are you achieving in this role? (Without being super specific – for example: "I am speaking to large and small groups." Or "I am influencing others to make a difference for a cause.")

19. What skills that you have are you using in this role?

20. What skills that you do not yet have, but would like to gain, when in this role?

REFERENCES

Chapter 1

1. Kirk Hallahan, Derina Holtzhausen, Betteke van Ruler, Dejan Verčič & Krishnamurthy Sriramesh(2007) Defining Strategic Communication, International Journal of Strategic Communication, 1:1, 3-35, DOI: 10.1080/15531180701285244

2. The Arthur W. Page Society Website. https://page.org/thought-leadership/building-belief

Chapter 3

1. Scott Jeffrey. "7 Steps To Discover Your Personal Core Values. Website. https://scottjeffrey.com/personal-core-values/

Chapter 4

1. Brené Brown. "Courage Is A Heart Word (and a Family Affair)." PBS Parents Website. http://www.pbs.org/parents/experts/archive/2010/11/courage-is-a-heart-word-and-a.html

Chapter 7

1. Michael D. Watkins. The First 90 Days. Harvard Business School Publishing: Boston, MA. 2013.

Creating Your Career Vision Exercise

1. StrengthsFinder
    https://www.gallup.com/press/176429/strengthsfinder.aspx

IT'S ALL ABOUT THE JOURNEY!
An Introduction to the Executives Interviewed

◀

You may have stumbled into the communications career field, or you may have been on this path from the first time you wrote copy other people wanted to read. The ways people fall into communications are as varied as the roles within this function.

The same is true for me and the executives I interviewed for this book.

I wanted to see the world and all its possibilities. What better way to go than joining the military? My path was nowhere near a straight line, and I took more than a few missteps along the way.

And I have loved every minute of it! Every twist and turn has brought me to where I am now, running my own executive search firm that finds the best potential candidates in marketing and communications.

My military and professional connections have given me access to some of the most amazing communications practitioners in the world. When I decided to write this book, I knew that their collective wisdom and experience would add great richness and depth to any suggestions I had for career development.

So, without further ado, I'd like you to know more about the career journeys and crossroads these executives took and what they love about being a communications leader.

From Sea To Shore

Naval Academy graduate David Albritton began his career on a U.S. Navy ship and later moved into the Navy Public Affairs community. After serving 10 years, he made the leap from military to corporate communications where he quickly moved up the ranks with each organization he joined.

David's ascension into the role of Chief Communications Officer for a brand new publicly traded Fortune 500 company is one that he reflects on as a favorite time in his career. When serving as the VP Communications for ITT Defense and Information Solutions, the company spun off and became Exelis. The entire executive team was starting fresh – all new at running a public company.

"It was a discovery opportunity for all of us," he recalled. The next three and a half years tested David in ways he had never been tested before and he rose to the challenges. "The way our entire team came together to accomplish a very challenging goal is something I'm most proud of," he said of the role and all he accomplished in it.

Today David is the Executive Director at General Motors where he works closely with the C-Suite on communications issues.

"I love that every day, you can't predict what the day is going to be like," David said as he described what he loves about being a communications leader. "A call from a reporter or an email can change my whole week. I enjoy that. I enjoy coming up with the narrative, having influence with executives, teaching why communications is so relevant to a company and showing what a difference we can make."

David Albritton, Executive Director
General Motors

An Accidental Love Affair

Steve Astle stumbled into communications and public relations early in his career, and completely by accident. He was teaching psychology at a university in Boston when a family friend who ran corporate communications for a large company invited Steve up to his office before going out to lunch.

Wide-eyed, Steve arrived at the beautiful office on the top floor of the tallest building in Boston and began meeting people in the communications profession. He became intrigued with this field, which he knew nothing about. After more research and lots of job applications – this was during a recession – someone at a public affairs agency took a chance on Steve and his communications career began.

Over the course of his career, Steve has held senior roles in agencies and in-house, and has worked with start-ups to Fortune 50 companies in a variety of industries. His natural curiosity and drive to continually learn and grow has been a critical element of his success.

"Communications has been my ticket to learning about many different things," he said. "I have a short attention span, but because I'm in communications, I haven't had to change my career every time I develop new interests. My fundamental skills and business acumen continue to improve even as I pursue new challenges and opportunities."

Steve Astle, Senior Vice President
Text100

A Foundation In Politics

Cory Curtis began his career in politics, where he always had an interest, first in Washington, D.C. and then in Seattle and Olympia. He never took any communications classes in college where he earned his degree in International Affairs, but he always felt it was a natural fit.

With an insatiable curiosity, Curtis' career toggled between politics, nonprofit and corporate communications roles at the senior most levels. His career has included serving as Director of Communications for Washington Governor Christine Gregoire, being the general manager for the Seattle office of Porter Novelli, and then leading the communications efforts for Intellectual Ventures. He's worked directly with renowned Founder/CEOs including Nathan Myhrvold and Pierre Omidyar.

Curtis believes that communications is a wildly misunderstood field where many people just hear the term "public relations" and have negative beliefs because they simply don't know what such a field encompasses. "We are forced to figure out answers on the fly.

I always loved speech and debate in school. You have 10 minutes to prepare and then provide a cohesive position," he said.

"There's a need for communications everywhere. Nonprofit, private and public sectors – there's a cool ability to cross platforms. A lot of careers don't give you that. There is the great mix of words and creativity.

It's very dynamic and I've had the opportunity to do some really interesting things from working with the Dalai Lama to helping the Governor communicate through the biggest economic crisis of our lifetime. Few other careers offer those opportunities."

Cory Curtis, Senior Director
Communications
The Omidyar Group

A Global Awakening

Ann Marie Gothard thought she was going to go to law school, but then her mother left a corporate position to start her own public relations agency and offered Ann Marie a chance to join her. Realizing law school was not really the direction she wanted to go, she decided to give agency life a try.

She began on the operations side, but ultimately got involved with bringing in new business and account management, which ultimately led to crafting communications strategies for clients. She had found her calling. Once the agency sold, Ann Marie moved on to working her way up in corporate and nonprofit organizations. Today, she leads the global media relations team

Henry Schein in New York.

What Ann Marie loves about this function is the strategy of words. "I see words like a mathematician sees numbers," she said. "Finding the essence of the situation, figuring out the right way to convey the message so it resonates with the audience to educate or inform, evoke an emotion, or help make a decision are my motivating factors."

Ann Marie Gothard, Vice President Corporate Media Relations Henry Schein

Translating Value Into Organizations and Beyond

With an educational foundation in business, Jason Hunke found his career calling was in communications and that started with his love for writing and storytelling. He began in the film and music industry doing publicity, but over the years his career journey evolved to blend of both agency and corporate leadership roles.

When he landed a role working with Vulcan, his communications expertise shifted to working with high profile and ultra-high net worth families. Since then, he has been sought after for roles within this specialty, including leading communications for Jackson Family Wines and now the Bill & Melinda Gates Foundation.

"Our field is an interesting intersection of business problem solving, creativity and how you engage with the business and the people," Jason said. "Communications ultimately delivers value across functions. We help translate issues, business and customer needs, products… whether it's in philanthropy, entertainment, government, CPG, you name the sector, we ultimately help translate something for people to move a needle on behavior. And that is fascinating."

Jason Hunke, Director
Employee and Executive Communications
Bill & Melinda Gates Foundation

Getting In On The Ground Floor

Michelle Jones was 15 years into her career before getting tapped for her first official communications role—and that position was the Vice President of marketing and communications. Having "grown up" in the company that recognized her communications skills, Michelle began as a computer programmer, moved into project work and eventually sales leadership.

Because the organization was fairly small, there was significant opportunity to prove your skills and move around. She describes her career journey as not one event, but a series of events that eventually led her to being tapped by company leaders for a branding and repositioning project that gave her the top communications job.

From the start, Michelle discovered the connection between employees, customers, investors and how all of it drives business results. Because of the various jobs she held, she learned how each department ran their business—and understanding the business is what makes Michelle a great communications executive.

Having impact on the business and people is what Michelle points to as the reason she loves this work. "You can have an impact on the work that your company is doing—impact on reputation, impact on profitable growth, people who are buying your products or services, people coming to work and staying at your company," she said. "You have to know all of your audiences and what drives them, what they will react to, the reputation drivers for the company, the value proposition."

Michelle Jones, Former SVP
Chief Communications
and Investor Officer CH2M
(acquired by Jacobs)

The Power Of Storytelling

Marta Newhart is another communications executive whose path was not an obvious one from the start. Right out of college, she joined The Boeing Company to work in sales, contracts and procurement.

At one point she was working on normalized trading status for China due to the huge impact the opposite would have on Boeing's ability to sell airplanes to China. In that process she worked on a grass roots campaign that included meeting the Secretary of Commerce, and Nancy Pelosi, Maxine Waters and several other high-ranking congressional members.

That's when the SVP of Communications took notice. "She told me that what I had done was create a communications plan," Marta said. "She offered me a job on her team and I almost didn't take it. My colleagues on the sales team, many of them were Chinese men, told me that I would be crazy to join Communications because aircraft sales was so prestigious."

Fast forward 20 years and Marta has held the role of Chief Communications Officer at three global companies. A natural story teller, she sees her challenge as a communications leader is to give good counsel to her CEO and colleagues and demonstrate how stories aren't just useful tools for entertainment and customer engagement. They are also a powerful way to change employees' mindsets and foster great connection within the business.

What Marta loves about communications is deeply rooted in her upbringing in a Mexican culture. "As a child I was told not to speak Spanish but to speak perfect English. Since I was around Spanish speaking people, I had to train myself to focus intently on the English-speaking people—what they said, how they said it. At a very young age I was a student of communication and I didn't even know it."

Marta Newhart,
Fortune 500 Chief Communications
Officer

The Importance Of Social Responsibility

John Onoda moved into corporate communications after being a newspaper reporter. For him, it was a matter of economics. He and his wife wanted to start a family, and he needed to earn more money.

But he was nearly fired his first year in when he was pulled aside by a colleague and told he couldn't be a reporter and write straight up news stories with all the warts, he needed to be a company advocate in his writing. He paid attention and his career took off.

John has held the top communications job for several big brands including Levi Strauss, General Motors, Visa and Charles Schwab. A big part of several roles included corporate social responsibility. "I love that I lucked into a job that very well suits my natural skills," John said. "We (in communications) are incredibly important and a powerful force for good in the world."

A long-time member of the Arthur W. Page Society, John is known not only for his communications expertise but also as a mentor and coach to many in the field. He loves helping individuals and organizations navigate through tough challenges ranging from new bosses, executive management who may not understand the value of communications, budgetary restraints, underperforming staffs, unrealistic goals, broken corporate cultures, and more.

John Onoda, Senior Consultant
Gagen MacDonald

In It from the Beginning

Krista Todd was recognized as someone who was going to excel in communications from the early stages in her career. From her first communications course in college to a career in both agency and in-house corporate communications roles, Krista quickly moved up the ladder.

Recruited to Logitech to be the succession plan to the Vice President, Krista was only 11 years out of college when she was tapped to come in and learn the ropes to take the helm in a few years. She proved herself as a leader and strategic thinker and on schedule, took over the global communications team at Logitech.

Krista's pull toward this field is all about the variety offered as a communications leader. "My job is new and exciting experiences everyday. It does make life more interesting," she said. "The industry changes, the company you work at changes, the world evolves, technology changes, the ways in which we can communicate with our publics changes. This all means that I must change, adapt, grow, learn and push myself regularly. I love that."

Krista Todd, Vice President
Communications
Logitech

A Labor Of Love

Donna Uchida began college on a full music scholarship, but then she volunteered on a congressional campaign for a neighbor whom she liked and respected, rather than having a desire to be in politics. It was here that she had the chance to work with people who truly understood the power of communications and how you could influence and move people to action. It was also when she learned she enjoyed writing more than playing violin.

While she lost her scholarship to pursue a degree in communications, she gained a career that she is truly passionate about. Today she works directly with the CEO and Chairman of Kaiser Permanente, the large healthcare organization out of Oakland, Calif.

 "What I love most is being able to see the impact that communications has on driving results—business results, reputation results or protecting a company from certain risks," Uchida said. "You have the opportunity as a communications leader to go far beyond what's on a typical communications job description and really expand to be the leader who connects people together, understands the bigger picture, and pulls in the right stakeholders to be able to build the vision of where we are going, bring in the teams to mobilize and be aligned, and feel really good about where we are going and what they are contributing."

Donna Uchida,
C-Suite Strategist

ABOUT THE AUTHOR

I began my career as a communicator in an unexpected venue—
the U.S. Army.

As a junior in high school, I was selected to be the editor of our
school newspaper, and I began writing for public consumption.
Combine that with a strong desire to bust out of Iowa and see the
world, I joined the Army as a journalist with my first duty station
being in Germany.

Just what I needed to figure out how little I knew of the world!

At the risk of aging myself, it was the Cold War era, long before
the United States was facing two simultaneous wars in the
Middle East. The stories and photos I produced were all about
training. I got my first taste of what I later learned was "executive
communications" when I interviewed the Division Commander
(a Brigadier General) and wrote his regular column for our base
newspaper.

It was during this assignment that I was asked by an officer, who
thought I "had potential," if I planned to go to college. I smugly
thought, "Why would I need college, when I have all this great
Army training as a journalist?" Even remembering this moment

makes me laugh—and turn red admitting my naiveté.

That officer gently suggested I look at journalists I admired and find out if they went to college, in case it might be something I would consider at the end of my enlistment. To this day, I am grateful for that conversation, as it led me on a career path that would never have been possible without his leadership and guidance.

After four years in the Army, I went on to the University of Missouri Journalism School in Columbia, MO. I thought journalism would be the road I traveled, imagining a life in New York working for a major magazine. But alas, a summer internship with *Travel & Leisure*, while spectacular, showed me that magazine editor and the Big Apple probably weren't going to be the perfect match for me.

During my senior year in college, I was constantly hanging out in the career center at the J-School, looking at opportunities and considering the endless possibilities of where I could end up. (This is the beginning of a theme that will repeat itself throughout my career.)

One day I saw a bulletin about a major company coming to the J-School to recruit for their Communicator Development Program (CDP). The headline for the posting made it seem like an advertising job—which was definitely not me—but for some reason I attended the presentation the day before the interviews for prospective candidates. This is where I learned about corporate communications. And this is the direction I knew I wanted for my future.

The only problem—all the interview spots were filled. Somehow, I talked my way into having the representative from the company add an extra half hour to her day, and she included me in the lineup. My first job out of college was as a CDP at The Dow Chemical Company.

What an exceptional start to a communicator's career this turned out to be! It was at Dow that I witnessed amazing communications leadership. I may have been wide-eyed and innocent to the ways of corporate life, but people I worked with genuinely seemed to love being there.

Nearly every person I worked for was thoughtful in their leadership style. They mentored, coached, encouraged. They didn't make life easy, but they made it interesting. I was a sponge, and my hard work paid off in great assignments and the opportunity to work on Silver Anvil* winning programs.

While all this was going on, I maintained my military affiliation by staying in the National Guard in both Missouri and Michigan as a journalist, earning my way up to Staff Sergeant, before applying for a direct commission in the U.S. Navy Reserve where I transitioned to becoming a Navy Public Affairs Officer.

Eventually my career wandering eye got the best of me, and I decided that moving on to a bigger city with more single twenty-somethings like myself was a good idea. My motivation was lifestyle in my personal life. I accepted a position at a well-respected, large PR agency—a career move that turned out to be a total mismatch.

I convinced myself the inner voice that said "think twice before taking this job" was just noise. Unfortunately, I didn't pay attention to the signs and within days in the new role, I knew I had made a serious career misstep.

Shortly after my one-year anniversary, I made a concerted effort to get off the bumpy road I found myself on and get back on a path where I knew I could be more successful. Those were valuable lessons I learned—first, to pay attention to your instincts when considering a job move, and next, to understand that just because an organization is recognized as an ideal place to work doesn't mean it's right for everyone.

You can be great, but not a great match for every company. It's okay to say no (or to leave) when something is not a fit.

It was at this crossroads that I made a giant leap which would lead me down a very different path for the rest of my life, though I didn't know it at the time. I chose to follow a dream I had of working on a cruise ship. Crazy, right?

When I was 14 years old, my parents took me to the Virgin Islands for vacation. This Iowa girl had never seen the ocean, and I certainly had never seen a cruise ship, of which there were a few in port in St. Thomas. When I got home from that vacation, I went straight to the public library and researched every cruise line I could find.

Back then, there weren't that many. I wrote to them all, explaining that I was 14 years old and wanted to know what kinds of jobs and what kind of education you needed to get a job on a cruise line. No one responded.

If you ask my mother about this story, she will tell you that she should have known then that my career would wind up being in recruiting or career coaching. She says, "Angee always liked figuring out how to get a job more than actually having one."

So, I packed my bags, sold my car and went aboard the Royal Viking Sun, number one cruise ship in the world according to Berlitz in 1992. My title was Skald Editor, writing a daily publication with features and interviews, not typically the kind of newsletter on cruise lines.

The ship went around the world, rarely hitting the same place twice in a year. While my work was not a journalistic piece of art, my wanderlust was honored. I had incredible experiences and developed lifelong friendships that still exist today.

It was on the ship that I took inventory of my life and career, knowing this was not a "forever job." What did I really want to do? After several self-assessments and reading books like *What Color is Your Parachute?* I figured out that, indeed, I really did like helping others with their career. After three years of sailing around the world, I moved to California to go to graduate school to earn my Master of Arts Degree in Career Development.

I needed a job while in school and found myself at a staffing agency in hopes of landing a J.O.B., instead of staying in PR where I knew the hours were long and the work unpredictable. As I sat across from the recruiter at this boutique agency, I quipped, "I bet I'd be good at what you do." She smiled, raised an eyebrow and introduced me to her boss. My recruiting career was born.

The next segment of my career journey is really all about the combination of doing communications work and being a recruiter and career coach.

I served part-time as a Navy Public Affairs Officer, where the work included everything from serving as the commanding officer of a small public affairs team during weekend drills to doing media training for senior officers to going on incredible assignments like joining a Navy Medical team in Nicaragua for an exercise that provided medical and dental care in rural areas of the country.

My "part-time" job also included being recalled to active duty after September 11, 2001, and creating an internal communications program for the Sixth Fleet family members so that they would be informed when the ships were deployed during a crisis.

My "other life" allowed me to move from agency recruiting to corporate in-house recruiting and recruiting program management to recruiting operations. Once again, I found myself in a highly desired company, but in a job where I was misaligned. My strengths were on the backburner, and I spent my days struggling through spreadsheets, program management and office politics.

It wasn't until a leader I respected saw my struggles and suggested I take what I had learned from the Strengths Finder exercise we did as a team and create my vision for the future.

In 2008 Linsey Careers was born.

When I created my company, I knew I wanted to work with marketing and communications professionals. This is a world I understood and was filled with people I enjoy being around. The mix of work I've been doing since the beginning is a heavy dose of recruiting, primarily senior communications leadership roles, as well as career coaching, both formally and informally.

With all the twists and turns my career took leading me to this point, I have very few (if any) regrets. Even those moments of misalignment led me to this place where I am doing work I love, helping companies figure out what they really need in a communications leader and making sure they find it. I'm also helping individuals achieve their career goals. I couldn't ask for more than that!

CPSIA information can be obtained
at www.ICGtesting.com
Printed in the USA
LVHW080031120119
603621LV00011B/27/P

9 781947 937772